Natural History Verse

An Anthology

Natural History Verse

An Anthology

CHOSEN
AND WITH AN INTRODUCTION
BY GERRY COTTER

CHRISTOPHER HELM

LONDON

© 1988 Introduction and selection Gerry Cotter
Illustrations by Terry Morgan
Christopher Helm (Publishers) Ltd, Imperial House,
21–25 North Street, Bromley, Kent BR1 1SD

ISBN 0–7470–0411–0

A CIP catalogue record for this book is available from the
British Library

Typeset by Paston Press, Loddon, Norfolk
Printed and bound in Great Britain by
Biddles Ltd, Guildford, Surrey

CONTENTS

[v]

CONTENTS

[vi]

Section 2 · PLANTS AND TREES

CONTENTS

Section 5 · SEASONS

CONTENTS

Section 6 · LANDSCAPE

[x]

CONTENTS

Section 7 · WATER AND ITS INHABITANTS

[xi]

Section 8 · MISCELLANEOUS

CONTENTS

For Jean

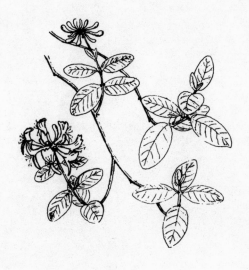

Natural History Verse

An Anthology

INTRODUCTION

Nature poetry has been a part of English Literature since its earliest days. Such a wide range of poems has been described as 'nature' poetry, however, the term can only ever be a rather vague one. This is because the word 'nature' itself has a number of different meanings, all of which may be included under the term 'nature poetry'. A nature poem may, for example, be a straightforward description of some part of the natural world, or it may be one in which nature is seen as some kind of deity. It may deal with our relationship with our environment, or with the relationship between nature and God. It may be concerned with human nature, concerned perhaps with the poet's perception and understanding of our place in the world. If all of these themes — and there are a good many more besides — can encompass 'nature poetry', the term must always be a general one.

In this anthology the poems I have looked for are those which have something to say about some aspect of the natural world. The contents are for the most part specifically 'natural history poetry' rather than generalised 'nature poetry', and with such an emphasis many fine nature poems have been excluded. The reader may wonder, perhaps, at the omission of such works as Wordsworth's *Tintern Abbey* and *Intimations of Immortality*, but although they are certainly nature poems their concern is with mankind first and the natural world second; there are a number of exceptions, but on the whole this is not a collection for anyone wanting to read poetry that reflects on our place in the universe. On the other hand, Hardy's *The Darkling Thrush* is specific enough to find a place, despite the fact that it is about doubt and hope, despair and faith, rather than the singing of a bird.

As I made my selection I looked in particular for poems which treat their subject with some originality of thinking, so that they are likely to make the reader perceive it in a fresh light; Ruth Pitter's beautiful *Dun-colour* is a good example of this:

[1]

>   ... but most beguiling,
> Perhaps because of the perfect shape, is the ash-dun,
> That quietest, most urbane, unprofaneable colour
> Reserved as her livery of beauty to the hedge-sparrow.

I have searched too for poems that make us realise the pleasure there is to be had from close observation of the world of nature. Various poets bring this home to us, but none more so than John Clare; his love of the countryside and its creatures shines through so much of his work, and I believe we can learn a lot from the country lore that he and other poets impart. Not for a moment does Clare set out to teach, but as we read him we realise the importance of sharp observation and we learn accordingly. What more pleasant way of learning about a nightingale's nest than to read Clare:

> How curious is the nest! no other bird
> Uses such loose materials, or weaves
> Its dwelling in such spots: dead oaken leaves
> Are placed without and velvet moss within,
> And little scraps of grass, and — scant and spare,
> Of what seem scarce materials — down and hair;
> For from men's haunts she nothing seems to win.

A small number of poems have been included because they are amusing, and it seems to me no bad thing to lighten the diet occasionally. Some of the poems, such as Wordsworth's *'I wandered lonely as a cloud'* and Keats's *Autumn* and *To a Nightingale*, will be very familiar, but I make no apologies for including them; an anthology such as this, it seemed to me, would just be incomplete without them. The greater part of the collection, though, should prove less familiar to most readers, and my hope is that it makes accessible some enjoyable poetry which many readers may otherwise have overlooked. I have tried to be as wide ranging in my choice as I could, so that the subject-matter covers many facets of the world of nature. Some species, though, simply do appear considerably more often in nature poetry than others; for centuries the nightingale has been the pre-eminent poetic bird, with the skylark and cuckoo not far behind, and it seemed only right that the anthology should reflect this.

Most of all, though, my aim has been to choose poetry that reflects the beauty — and sometimes the cruelty — of the natural world, whether it is about a snail or a sunset, a snipe or a snowstorm. It is, in short, an anthology for anyone who loves the world of nature.

Over the centuries the way in which nature has featured in poetry has changed very considerably, and in making my choice of verse I wanted the collection to bring this out. It is not by chance that the majority of the poems date from the beginning of the nineteenth century onwards, since before that time the number of poets who had apparently felt any great empathy with birds, animals and the rest of nature was very small. In simplistic terms, the poetic approach to nature changed at this time from a rather impersonal, detached one to a very personal, involved one, with Wordsworth being the dominant figure in the transition.

This impersonal attitude to nature may seem rather unreal to us today, but it had persisted for centuries. To be fair to the poets, they were doing no more than reflecting the feelings of their time, for the history of mankind's relationship with the 'lower' orders of animals is one that, to many modern eyes, does us little credit. In the first chapter of the Book of Genesis it was laid down that mankind shall 'have dominion over the fish of the sea, and over the fowl of the air, and over the cattle, and over all the earth, and over every creeping thing that creepeth upon the earth', and for many centuries western man tended to take that as his watchword. As it happened, a good many poets, being sensitive souls, wrote about nature, especially birds, with more sympathy than one might expect in view of this prevailing belief in human dominion; but by the standards of the last two centuries this sympathy was subdued, perhaps even artificial. Hardly ever before the eighteenth centry does a poet give the impression that he sees the birds he writes about as sentient creatures with their own lives to lead that should be looked at in a quite different way from the human race.

As a result of this impersonal attitude, nature poetry before the eighteenth century is generally formalised and stylised. Birds and animals are used as symbols, or as extensions of mankind, different species representing different moral values. It has its own attractiveness, to be sure, but it is some way removed from the kind of poetry that says something worthwhile about the natural world.

The earliest English poetry dates from Anglo-Saxon times, the nature element of it being mostly confined to birds and animals. In general they are mournful creatures, with cries redolent of sorrow and doom, although a more joyful picture does break through occasionally. Often they are presented in an unattractive light, some of them regularly being associated with battle and death. In one poem, for instance, the eagle, the raven and the wolf wait on the edge of a battle to feast upon the bodies; in another the gull is described as corpse-greedy. A number of the birds have supernatural associations, partly through their links with death and partly through the idea that their cries foretell the future; the cuckoo, with his 'woeful voice', is supposed to do this. This is hardly surprising since the supernatural was an important element in Anglo-Saxon life, and birds were often regarded as omens just as they had been in classical times. Down through the centuries there have, after all, been many superstitions connected with birds, and regarding them as possessing supernatural powers is really no more than a reflection of this.

Whether this is nature poetry in any meaningful sense of the term may well be a matter for debate. I like to think that it is; there may not be any attempt to empathise with the birds and animals but it does at least show us how they were regarded at the time. And to be aware of the attitudes prevailing at different times in the past must be an essential part of our understanding of our literature.

By medieval times the birds had come virtually to represent people, having human characteristics and moral values ascribed to them, to say nothing of the power of speech. In general, these characteristics are much as we might expect — the unfaithful cuckoo, the joyful nightingale — and some, such as the noble peregrine, still persist today. The idea of using birds as mouthpieces to discuss different aspects of human life, especially love, is likely to make us ask once again whether this can reasonably be called nature poetry, but there are some works which are rather more relevant to our theme. Chaucer's *Parliament of Fowls* is one such. The poet dreams that he meets the Goddess of Nature surrounded by a large assembly of birds, each of which is listed and characterised in a few words. His characterisations are based on the lore of the time, so that the kite is cowardly, the turtle dove faithful, the sparrow lecherous, and so on. It tells us nothing about the birds as real creatures, but once again it has its value in showing us the attitudes and beliefs of the period.

Medieval nature poetry is, then, emblematic and symbolic, as is much of medieval art. Some people in this era, however, were genuine nature watchers: Gerald of Wales, for example, was giving accurate descriptions of birds and fish at the end of the twelfth century. Not in poetry, it is true, but the important point is that the scientific observation of nature was beginning again after having been largely ignored for many centuries.

Nature poetry in Elizabethan times is mostly pastoral poetry. It is a world of permanent springtime, love-sick swains, beautiful maidens and glorious birdsong. The flowers are in bloom, blossom is on the trees, music is everywhere — especially in the throat of the nightingale, usually called Philomela from a story in Greek mythology. In general the verse is lighter in touch than in the preceding centuries, although many of the traditional bird characteristics, such as those set out in the *Parliament of Fowls*, are still in evidence.

If this brief summary of pastoral poetry has a slight tongue-in-cheek ring to it, it is because twentieth-centry cynicism tends to make it difficult for many of use to take it seriously. A poem called *Spring's Welcome* by John Lyly, who lived from 1553 to 1606, exemplifies the point:

> What bird so sings, yet so does wail?
> O 'tis the ravish'd nightingale,
> *Jug, jug, jug, jug, tereu*! she cries,
> And still her woes at midnight rise.
> Brave prick-song! Who is't now we hear?
> None but the lark so shrill and clear;
> Now at heaven's gate she claps her wings,
> The morn not waking till she sings.
> Hark, hark, with what a pretty throat
> Poor robin redbreast tunes his note!
> Hark how the jolly cuckoos sing
> *Cuckoo*! to welcome in the spring!
> *Cuckoo*! to welcome in the spring!

This is pleasant and melodious, but also, it seems to me, both artificial and superficial. The world of nature is painted, but it is hardly explored — not by the poets of the period, at least. As a result, pastoral poetry appears not to be the stuff to which many modern readers turn, and so it does not feature very largely in this anthology.

But if there was little depth to the poets' knowledge of the natural world, the sixteenth century was the time when the field naturalists, men like William Turner, began their studies in earnest. Once ornithology, zoology, botany and so on had been put on a proper scientific basis they gained many adherents, and inevitably this had the effect of making nature poetry at least slightly more realistic. But it was a slow process; even as late as the eighteenth century animals were often still the stereotypes of literary convention — the cunning fox, the provident ant, and suchlike — that they had been for centuries. The insistence on regarding wildlife in human terms also took a long time to dwindle away, both among the poets and the scientific writers.

By the eighteenth century the poetry had grown less and less a product of the poets' vivid imaginations and more and more to reflect the real world of nature. This was the age of reason and the age of elegance, which meant an end of the fanciful poetic conceits, an emphasis on careful observation, and a literary style that was polished and polished again. The central nature poem of the eighteenth century, which illustrates all of these points, is Thomson's *The Seasons*, published in 1730 and considerably revised in 1744. This can lay claim to being the most influential nature poem ever written since in it, virtually for the first time, wild creatures are treated as wild creatures and not as some element of human life. In Spring, for instance, a fairly comprehensive account of the birds' breeding season is given, while in Autumn mention is made of their migrations. If Thomson's style is somewhat over-sentimental for modern taste, we can forgive him when we remember the influence he had on poets such as John Clare.

Yet throughout the eighteenth century the feeling persists that the poets are not really personally involved with the creatures about which they are writing. The wealth of detail in *The Seasons* was generally not echoed in other nature poetry, and what detail there is tends to be presented in an objective, impersonal manner. In fact this impersonal manner is true even of *The Seasons* itself, since Thomson keeps his own direct involvement very much to a minimum.

Only with the Romantics does the poetry become personal, as the poet regularly puts himself into his verse. The poet as passive observer is replaced by the poet as active participant, and the man most responsible for this was William Wordsworth. One tends to think of Wordsworth as the high priest of nature poetry, and certainly his influence, stretching over much of the nineteenth century and even into the twentieth, was very extensive; but his importance can be, and has been, exaggerated. His most profound poetry generally deals with landscape and the elements, for having spent countless hours walking the hills in all sorts of weathers, his intimacy with their grandeur gives him a splendid foundation for his reflections on the human situation. When he writes about birds and flowers, though, he has less scope for profundity, since a cuckoo or a daisy simply doesn't have the ability to inspire deep thoughts in the way that a mountain landscape does, although Wordsworth does his best to suggest that they are something out of the ordinary. Precisely because of this the majority of his poems in the following pages deal with birds and flowers, since deep thoughts on the human condition are not what I looked for when making my choice.

Because he is an active participant in the natural world, in much of Wordsworth's writing there is an interchange between man and nature. An excellent example of this is '*I wandered lonely as a cloud*', which may have become ultra-familiar but has done so only because it is a good poem. As it opens, the poet is alone, while the daffodils are described in human terms — 'a crowd/A host', 'dancing'. The various natural elements are then interlinked, as the flowers are compared to the stars in the sky and the waves dance just as the flowers did. But the sky contains clouds as well as stars, so what could be more natural than the lonely poet finding himself drawn into the tableau? By the end, when he is solitary (no longer lonely, note) his heart 'dances with the daffodils', and man and nature are unified. Seeking to create, and understand, unity between mankind and nature is a fundamental element of Wordsworth's verse.

The birds and flowers about which Wordsworth wrote are mostly familiar species, those that had figured prominently in nature poetry for centuries. This is true of the other Romantic poets also, but the reason why Keats's *To a Nightingale* and Shelley's *To a Skylark* are much more widely known than earlier poems on the same species is that their treatment is quite unlike anything that had gone before. In earlier bird poetry one often has the feeling that the bird is little more than, say, a toy in a music box or a cuckoo in a clock, but with the Romantics the birds become almost magical creatures, sometimes even immortal ones. In fact the reader may well feel that they are every bit as unrealistic as the earlier stereotypes, in which case it should be remembered that painting a realistic picture was not the poet's aim. What is important is the poet's state of mind, for he is using the natural world as the territory for an exploration of human experience. Birds are especially useful for this; since it is often difficult to link the song that one hears to a particular singer, the poet can suggest that the 'disembodied' voice of the bird could be the voice of nature itself, or perhaps almost a voice from another world. The nightingale and the skylark are ideal for this as both are often hidden from view — the nightingale in darkness and the lark too high up. I said earlier that I have mostly avoided poetry which is concerned with the exploration of human experience, but where a poem has a specific subject and is an enjoyable one I have sometimes bent my rules.

If it is realism that is desired the poet who provides it is John Clare. He was exactly contemporary with Shelley and Keats, but his verse has none of the Romantic excesses that characterise theirs. Born of peasant stock in Northamptonshire and with only a scant education, he is a countryman to his fingertips who writes about the countryside and its creatures with enormous knowledge and a love that clearly runs very deep indeed. Clare is by some margin the major contributor to this volume, for he is beyond any doubt the finest naturalist of all our poets, giving a whole string of observations on hitherto unrecorded aspects of bird behaviour and many careful descriptions of nests and eggs. Over 140 species of birds and almost as many plants appear in his writings (a good proportion of them first records for his county), which is a much higher total than any other poet can claim. And it is all done with such freshness and delight; the words 'I love' occur over and over again in his verse.

As with all the leading naturalists his eye for detail is extremely acute, and it is clear that he is no mere observer of nature but someone who becomes quite lost and absorbed in it. This gives his verse real immediacy, sometimes even a cinematic quality. *The Nightingale's Nest* is a good example of this, with Clare taking the role of leading us in search of the nest that today would belong to David Attenborough and a television film crew. Undoubtedly the television viewer does gain over the reader of poetry in terms of visual experience — but does he or she not lose out on the pleasure of exercising the imagination?

When compared to Wordsworth, Clare acquits himself very creditably. Wordsworth, of course, was a man of culture and intellect who sought always to explore the mysticism that he felt to be ever present in nature. In doing this, birds and flowers were often imbued with a greater significance than most people would give them, and whether this enlargement is altogether successful must be a matter of opinion. Clare, much more intimate with wild creatures than Wordsworth every was, simply described what he saw as he saw it, a very distinctive voice wanting to share his profound love of nature with us all. If Clare could not compete with Wordsworth as the philosopher of nature, Wordsworth certainly could not compete with Clare as the poet of the countryside.

Clare's opinion of Keats is worth noting in passing, since the point he makes could apply to a good many other nature poets over the centuries:

> His descriptions of scenery are often very fine but as is the case with other inhabitants of great cities he often described nature as she appeared to his fancies and not as he would have described her had he witnessed the things he describes.

Admittedly this does, as it stands, suggest that Clare had not appreciated some of the finer points of Keats's poetry, but one feels that there is an element of truth in it all the same.

As he grew older Clare's verse often became bitter. Partly this reflects his frustration at lack of further success after his first volume had been well received, but it is also very much related to the Enclosure Movement. In order to improve the agricultural yield of the land the countryside was transformed — trees, sometimes whole coppices, were cut down, fences appeared around commons, streams were diverted and so on. It was accompanied by a social upheaval that was deep and far reaching, especially in the first two decades of the nineteenth century. Northamptonshire was one of the areas most affected, so that in a short period it changed dramatically; and as Clare's attachment to his native county was very intense the changes appalled him. This, of course, was reflected in his poetry, and explains why a poem such as *Badger*, with its bitterness of tone, can appear amongst others in which the phrase 'I love' occurs with great frequency.

To my knowledge, no study has been published on the effects of the Enclosure Movement on the writing of nature poetry. At the end of the eighteenth and beginning of the nineteenth centuries large areas of the Midlands, East Anglia and the northern Home Counties were radically altered, and this may have affected a good deal of the verse that was written at the time. For those readers who like to set literature against its social background, it is worth remembering that this period saw more change in the English countryside than any other until the Second World War.

Clare was especially unfortunate in that as his poetic powers matured public interest in nature poetry declined, consigning him to poverty and ultimately to madness. As more and more was learned about the natural world prose steadily took over as the obvious medium in which to write about it, and while some of Clare's writings are in prose they have none of the ease and charm of his verse and were not published in his lifetime.

The rise of nature prose writing did not for a moment spell the end of nature poetry, though. Prose was the obvious medium for recording the scientific discoveries that were being made, but the poets were still very active. Not surprisingly, the post-Romantic writers settled down into a style less excessive than that of their predecessors, tending towards realism but without the minute attention to detail of Clare. This synthesis of Romanticism and realism is often a happy one, with some very enjoyable nature poetry being produced.

Increasing scientific awareness meant that some of the exotic creatures which had found favour with earlier poets were abandoned. Instead, the emphasis was on the everyday species, with the thrush and the blackbird featuring prominently in bird poetry for the first time. The period also saw a considerable increase in the number of species taken for the subject of poems, a trend that has continued to the present day.

Within this general framework the differences among the nature poets can be striking. Tennyson, for example, can at times excel at depicting the landscape of the English countryside with much richness of detail. Wordsworthian mysticism has little place in this, for underlying his poetry is the Victorian preoccupation with scientific study. Because of this he is aware of the cruel side of nature and makes frequent reference to it; nature 'knows nothing', he says, and kills without knowing that it is happening. This is something the Romantics had tended to ignore, but it is a theme that is taken up by a number of later writers, Hardy in particular. Tennyson cannot claim, though, to be a major nature poet. He possessed enormous poetic gifts and he wrote copiously, but somehow there is nothing distinctive about his nature verse. In the words of Edmund Blunden in his *Nature in English Literature* 'his pastoral . . . drifted into a compilation of natural history jottings, to be thrust into his versification at a pinch'.

[10]

Altogether different was William Barnes, the Dorset poet who wrote much of his verse in the dialect of his county. The influence of Wordsworth may be traced in his work, although nature for him is usually cultivated countryside rather than dramatic mountains; he prefers the gentle beauties of the Blackmore Vale, with which he is familiar, to a confrontation that gives rise to profound philosophical reflections. As well as natural history subjects his poems deal with life in the local community, so that we are given a rounded picture of his particular corner of nineteenth-century Dorset.

He is often compared with Clare since both are such *rural* poets, but there are several differences between them. Barnes was altogether more sophisticated and his verse altogether more controlled and polished, whereas Clare summed himself up by saying 'I found the poems in the fields/ And only wrote them down'. Clare simply used dialect words because they came naturally to him, while Barnes took great care and deliberation over his Dorset dialect. If Clare is a realist, Barnes depicts his community in a way that is idealistic, sometimes almost idyllic. The musicality of the dialect gives Barnes's verse a charm that may well appeal to the reader who is looking for something a little out of the ordinary.

A more famous Dorset writer was, of course, Thomas Hardy, a man whose view of nature was very much less idealised than Barnes's. Through the popularity of his novels, Hardy's belief that nature is cruelly indifferent to human affairs has become widely known, and it is a theme that continues throughout his poetry. He is justifiably famed as a major nature writer, but in fact the greater part of his verse deals with human activities set against a background of the natural world; little of it is specifically the natural history poetry for which I was searching. Some of his poems, though, have great beauty and complexity, often much more so than one realises at a first reading. *The Fallow Deer at the Lonely House* is an excellent example, an exquisitely depicted scene that makes one wish he had written much more of its kind.

Other important nineteenth-century nature writers include Arnold, Patmore, Browning, Swinburne, Hopkins, Meredith and Bridges, although not all of them feature in the present collection. On the other side of the Atlantic, Bryant, Emerson, Thoreau, Whitman and Emily Dickinson all made significant contributions to the genre. Emerson, for example, saw the contemplation of nature as a means by which mankind could learn to worship God. His intense religious faith strove to come to terms with an equally intense belief in modern science, and the only way in which the two could be united, he believed, was through the symbol. It was to nature that he turned for his symbols, trying to go beyond what he saw and heard to reach out to the spirit that he felt runs through all the various forms of nature. His belief was that the task of the poet was to link the laws of nature with the laws of morality, thereby bringing religion and science together; in this way he was able to make the connection between the everyday life of the woods and fields on the one hand and the philosophical notion of 'universal nature' on the other. The verse which illustrates this best is not included in this collection, but a poem such as *The Snowstorm*, with its rich visual images, shows how natural laws correspond to the laws of God. The idealism inherent in his work was echoed by his close associate Thoreau and later by Whitman.

The first important nature poet who wrote only in the twentieth century was Edward Thomas, a writer whose poetic flowering was tragically cut short by his death in the First World War. His landscape was the gentle hills of Wiltshire and Hampshire, a district of quiet corners and meandering paths, in his day at least. What particularly attracted him were the things that other people overlooked, the dark old combe or the nettles in the corner of the farmyard, and his way of drawing them to our attention is through verse that is direct and uncomplicated.

Thomas was fortunate in that he was encouraged by one of the major figures of twentieth-century American poetry, Robert Frost. Frost himself wrote much nature poetry, though almost all of it has a strong human element; so much so, in fact, that he more than once denied he was a nature poet at all. As with Thomas his language is that of everyday speech, with archaic poetic diction very firmly rejected — a process which has become ever more widespread as the twentieth century has advanced.

This emphasis on 'naturalness' continues in the poetry of D. H. Lawrence. His style, often similar to that of Whitman, whom he admired, may appear at first sight to be unpolished and loosely structured, but this is deceptive. In fact his poetry is very specific, and he has a splendid empathy with and respect for the creatures about which he writes. *Kangaroo* is a fine example of this; he has obviously watched the animal closely, and the poem, in essence, explores the notion of what it is like actually to *be* a kangaroo —

which is, perhaps, the ultimate in nature poetry. By contrast, in *Snake*, one of the finest of all nature poems, man and the natural world are in confrontation — and it is very significant that it is the *educated* voice within the man that urges him to commit the petty act of throwing a log at the departing snake, thereby destroying its dignity. The message is clear: nature is altogether greater than mankind, and the more we respect its beauty, its dignity, its vital life-force, the better chance we shall have of understanding it and learning from it. In his own way John Clare had said the same thing a century earlier, and what Lawrence was doing was bringing it into the twentieth century.

A crucial feature of twentieth-century life has been, of course, the decline in the number of people holding committed religious beliefs, and this has been reflected in the nature poetry that has been written; poems exploring the relationship between nature and God have been few and far between. Indeed, with Lawrence an element of paganism is sometimes discernible in his work, while Ted Hughes, in language that is stark and often brutal, writes about nature with an unprecedented fierceness. The keynote of twentieth-century nature poetry is realism; a different order of realism from Clare's detailed descriptions, perhaps, but a realistic reflection of the natural world as each poet sees it, based on their own personal encounters with it.

Those are the crucial words — 'as each poet sees it'. For nature is nature is nature, and all we can do, after all, is observe it, enjoy it, reflect upon it and, if we so choose, offer our interpretation of it to the world. If we happen to be one of those gifted people who can create good poetry, the world will have cause to be grateful to us.

The reader may remark on the omission of a number of good modern nature poets who might reasonably have been expected to feature in an anthology such as this. I had hoped to include poems by Andrew Young, Laurie Lee, William Carlos Williams, Gerald Bullett, Norman Nicholson, and various others, but I have not done so for one reason: the copyright permission fees requested by their publishers seemed to me excessive, and I declined to pay them.

Suggested Reading

Joseph Warren Beach: *The Concept of Nature in Nineteenth Century English Poetry* (Russell & Russell, New York)

Edmund Blunden: *Nature in English Literature* (Hogarth Press, London)

W. J. Keith: *The Poetry of Nature* (University of Toronto Press, Toronto)

Peggy Munsterberg (ed.): *Penguin Book of Bird Poetry* (Allen Lane, London) (The lengthy introduction gives a detailed account of the development of bird poetry)

Keith Thomas: *Man and the Natural World* (Penguin, Harmondsworth)

Section 1
BIRDS

Heron

On the edge of my dream a question
Poised,
Posed?
Eternal perhaps —
But no questions are eternal
As the plants bow towards the light.
Silent, still he stands there
Like a silver statue of some elder statesman, hunched
For the kill,
Or a priest about to deliver an absolution;
This philosopher's mind — I reflect — is full of
Absolutions
Or absolutes.
The golden dagger he was born with,
Heron, killer.

In the haze of a late afternoon in summer
He metamorphoses lazily,
All the time in this world and the next
To nod a path along the marshes.
Ardea cinerea
Even the name has a ring of spectre silver,
And curlew pipes infinity along.

My afternoons are full of ghosts
And my dreams are full of herons
Filling the warm air
Distilling the warm air with a prayer of sorts
And then bowing for the kill.

My dreams are full of herons dancing in the mud.
Crazy dreams.

BOB TURPIN

[17]

Bittern

Ham actress of the reeds —
Head thrown back in dramatic pose,
A frozen eternity of anguish
Stemmed from a moment's over-acting
Over-reacting, mere fear
The only justification.
What do you see as you stare upwards
In fear? Frozen eternity —
Or some universal melodrama
You can't understand?

Butterbump they used to call you,
Silly name, undignified,
But maybe they'd seen you
Slipping and sliding on ice,
Graceless clown; a real ham actress
Would never have taken a risk like that.
But then again, I seem to remember,
My friends and I often fell over
Last winter.

I can't conceive of what it's like
To be courted by booms — can it
Really be love when the whole world's
Reduced to an echoing hollow drum?
When the same sound expresses
Love, hope and fear, and a million
Emotions besides, then why do we bother,
You and I, to look out for eternity?
Why do we bother, you and I,
To search for some echoing truth?

But you know better than search for echoes
And hold your peace for all to hear;
You feel those drums and maybe
You smile inside — ham actress
You may be, but yet I wonder if,

[18]

Deep in your secret world, those hollow
Echoes take on some meaning after all
For those who understand
The silent code.

OWEN HARDY

The Silver Swan

The silver swan, who living had no note,
When death approached, unlocked her silent throat,
Leaning her breast against the reedy shore,
Thus sung her first and last, and sung no more:
'Farewell all joys! O death, come close mine eyes;
More geese than swans now live, more fools than wise.'

ORLANDO GIBBONS

The Dying Swan

I

The plain was grassy, wild and bare,
Wide, wild, and open to the air,
Which had built up everywhere
   An under-roof of doleful grey.
With an inner voice the river ran,
Adown it floated a dying swan,
   And loudly did lament.

[19]

It was the middle of the day.
Ever the weary wind went on,
   And took the reed-tops as it went.

II

Some blue peaks in the distance rose,
And white against the cold-white sky,
Shone out their crowning snows.
   One willow over the river wept,
And shook the wave as the wind did sigh;
Above in the wind was the swallow,
   Chasing itself at its own wild will,
   And far thro' the marish green and still
   The tangled water-courses slept,
Shot over with purple, and green, and yellow.

III

The wild swan's death-hymn took the soul
Of that waste place with joy
Hidden in sorrow: at first to the ear
The warble was low, and full and clear;
And floating about the under-sky,
Prevailing in weakness, the coronach stole
Sometimes afar, and sometimes anear;
But anon her awful jubilant voice,
With a music strange and manifold,
Flow'd forth on a carol free and bold;
As when a mighty people rejoice
With shawms, and with cymbals, and harps of gold,
And the tumult of their acclaim is roll'd
Thro' the open gates of the city afar,
To the shepherd who watcheth the evening star.
And the creeping mosses and clambering weeds,
And the willow-branches hoar and dank,
And the wavy swell of the soughing reeds,
And the wave-worn horns of the echoing bank,
And the silvery marish-flowers that throng
The desolate creeks and pools among,
Were flooded over with eddying song.

ALFRED, LORD TENNYSON

On Scaring Some Water Fowl

In Loch-Turit, A Wild Scene Among
The Hills of Ochtertyre

Why, ye tenants of the lake,
For me your wat'ry haunt forsake?
Tell me, fellow-creatures, why
At my presence thus you fly?
Why disturb your social joys,
Parent, filial, kindred ties? —
Common friend to you and me,
Nature's gifts to all are free:
Peaceful keep your dimpling wave,
Busy feed, or wanton lave;
Or, beneath the sheltering rock,
Bide the surging billow's shock.

Conscious, blushing for our race,
Soon, too soon, your fears I trace.
Man, your proud, usurping foe,
Would be lord of all below;
Plumes himself in Freedom's pride,
Tyrant stern to all beside.

The eagle, from the cliffy brow,
Marking you his prey below,
In his breast no pity dwells,
Strong Necessity compels.
But Man, to whom alone is giv'n
A ray direct from pitying Heav'n,
Glories in his heart humane —
And creatures for his pleasure slain.

In these savage, liquid plains,
Only known to wand'ring swains,
Where the mossy riv'let strays,
Far from human haunts and ways;
All on Nature you depend,
And life's poor season peaceful spend.

Or, if man's superior might
Dare invade your native right,

On the lofty ether borne,
Man with all his pow'rs you scorn;
Swiftly seek, on clanging wings,
Other lakes and other springs;
And the foe you cannot brave,
Scorn at least to be his slave.

ROBERT BURNS

Four Ducks on a Pond

Four ducks on a pond,
A grass-bank beyond,
A blue sky of spring,
White clouds on the wing;
What a little thing
To remember for years —
To remember with tears!

WILLIAM ALLINGHAM

Quack

What said the drake to his lady-love
    But *Quack*, then *Quack*, then QUACK!
And she, with long love-notes as sweet as his,
    Said *Quack* — then, softlier, QUACK
And Echo that lurked by the old red barn,
    Beyond their straddled stack,
Listening this love-lorn pair's delight,
    Quacked their quacked *Quack*, *Quack*, *Quacks* back.

WALTER DE LA MARE

'A sparrow-hawk proud'

A sparrow-hawk proud did hold in wicked jail
Music's sweet chorister, the nightingale;
To whom with sighs she said, 'O set me free,
And in my song I'll praise no bird but thee'.
The hawk replied, 'I will not lose my diet
To let a thousand such enjoy their quiet'.

ANON (*early 17th century*)

The Dalliance of the Eagles

Skirting the river road (my forenoon walk, my rest),
Skyward in air a sudden muffled sound, the dalliance of the eagles,
The rushing amorous contact high in space together,
The clinching, interlocking claws, a living, fierce, gyrating wheel,
Four beating wings, two beaks, a swirling mass tight grappling,
In tumbling, turning, clustering loops, straight downward falling,
Till o'er the river pois'd, the twain yet one, a moment's lull,
A motionless still balance in the air, then parting, talons loosing,
Upward again on slow-firm pinions slanting, their separate
    diverse flight,
She hers, he his, pursuing.   WALT WHITMAN

The Eagle

Fragment

He clasps the crag with crookëd hands;
Close to the sun in lonely lands,
Ringed with the azure world, he stands.

The wrinkled sea beneath him crawls;
He watches from his mountain walls,
And like a thunderbolt he falls.

ALFRED, LORD TENNYSON

[23]

The Windhover

To Christ our Lord

I caught this morning morning's minion, king-
  dom of daylight's dauphin, dapple-dawn-drawn Falcon, in his
    riding
  Of the rolling level underneath him steady air, and striding
High there, how he rung upon the rein of a wimpling wing
In his ecstasy! then off, off forth on swing,
  As a skate's heel sweeps smooth on a bow-bend: the hurl and
    gliding
  Rebuffed the big wind. My heart in hiding
Stirred for a bird, — the achieve of, the mastery of the thing!

Brute beauty and valour and act, oh, air, pride, plume, here
  Buckle! AND the fire that breaks from thee then, a billion
Times told lovelier, more dangerous. O my chevalier!

  No wonder of it: shéer plód makes plough down sillion
Shine, and blue-bleak embers, ah my dear,
  Fall, gall themselves, and gash gold-vermilion.

GERARD MANLEY HOPKINS

The Black Vulture

Aloof upon the day's immeasured dome,
    He holds unshared the silence of the sky.
    Far down his bleak, relentless eyes descry
The eagle's empire and the falcon's home —
Far down, the galleons of sunset roam;
    His hazards on the sea of morning lie;
    Serene, he hears the broken tempest sigh
Where cold sierras gleam like scattered foam.

And least of all he holds the human swarm —
    Unwitting now that envious men prepare
    To make their dream and its fulfillment one,
When, poised above the caldrons of the storm,
    Their hearts, contemptuous of death, shall dare
    His roads between the thunder and the sun.

GEORGE STERLING

The Hawk

The hawk slipt out of the pine, and rose in the sunlit air:
Steady and still he poised; his shadow slept on the grass:
And the bird's song sickened and sank: she cowered with furtive
    stare
Dumb, till the quivering dimness should flicker and shift and pass.

Suddenly, down he dropped: she heard the hiss of his wing,
Fled with a scream of terror: oh, would she had dared to rest!
For the hawk at eve was full, and there was no bird to sing,
And over the heather drifted the down from a bleeding breast.

A. C. BENSON

[25]

Hurt Hawks

I

The broken pillar of the wing jags from the clotted shoulder,
The wing trails like a banner in defeat,
No more to use the sky forever but live with famine
And pain a few days: cat nor coyote
Will shorten the week of waiting for death, there is game without
talons.
He stands under the oak-bush and waits
The lame feet of salvation; at night he remembers freedom
And flies in a dream, the dawns ruin it.
He is strong and pain is worse to the strong, incapacity is worse.
The curs of the day come and torment him
At distance, no one but death the redeemer will humble that head,
The intrepid readiness, the terrible eyes.
The wild God of the world is sometimes merciful to those
That ask mercy, not often to the arrogant.
You do not know him, you communal people, or you have
forgotten him;
Intemperate and savage, the hawk remembers him;
Beautiful and wild, the hawks, and men that are dying, remember him.

II

I'd sooner, except the penalties, kill a man than a hawk; but the
great redtail
Had nothing left but unable misery
From the bone too shattered for mending, the wing that trailed
under his talons when he moved.
We had fed him six weeks, I gave him freedom,
He wandered over the foreland hill and returned in the evening,
asking for death,
Not like a beggar, still eyed with the old
Implacable arrogance. I gave him the lead gift in the twilight.
What fell was relaxed,
Owl-downy, soft feminine feathers; but what
Soared: the fierce rush: the night-herons by the flooded river
cried fear at its rising
Before it was quite unsheathed from reality.

ROBINSON JEFFERS

[26]

Eagle in New Mexico

Towards the sun, towards the south-west
A scorched breast.
A scorched breast, breasting the sun like an answer,
Like a retort.

An eagle at the top of a low cedar-bush
On the sage-ash desert
Reflecting the scorch of the sun from his breast;
Eagle, with the sickle dripping darkly above.

Erect, scorched-pallid out of the hair of the cedar,
Erect, with the god-thrust entering him from below,
Eagle gloved in feathers
In scorched white feathers
In burnt dark feathers
In feathers still fire-rusted;
Sickle-overswept, sickle dripping over and above.

Sun-breaster.
Staring two ways at once, to right and left;
Masked one
Dark-visaged
Sickle-masked
With iron between your two eyes;
You feather-gloved
To the feet;
Foot-fierce;
Erect one;
The god-thrust entering you steadily from below.

You never look at the sun with your two eyes.
Only the inner eye of your scorched broad breast
Looks straight at the sun.

You are dark
Except scorch-pale-breasted;
And dark cleaves down and weapon-hard downward curving

[27]

At your scorched breast,
Like a sword of Damocles,
Beaked eagle.

You've dipped it in blood so many times
That dark face-weapon, to temper it well,
Blood-thirsty bird.

Why do you front the sun so obstinately,
American eagle?
As if you owed him an old, old grudge, great sun: or an old,
   old allegiance.

When you pick the red smoky heart from a rabbit or a
   light-blooded bird
Do you lift it to the sun, as the Aztec priests used to lift red
   hearts of men?

Does the sun need steam of blood do you think
In America, still,
Old eagle?

Does the sun in New Mexico sail like a fiery bird of prey in the sky
Hovering?

Does he shriek for blood?
Does he fan great wings above the prairie, like a hovering,
   blood-thirsty bird?

And are you his priest, big eagle
Whom the Indians aspire to?
Is there a bond of bloodshed between you?

Is your continent cold from the ice-age still, that the sun
   is so angry?
Is the blood of your continent somewhat reptilian still,
That the sun should be greedy for it?

I don't yield to you, big, jowl-faced eagle.
Nor you nor your blood-thirsty sun

That sucks up blood
Leaving a nervous people.

Fly-off, big bird with a big black back.
Fly slowly away, with a rust of fire in your tail,
Dark as you are on your dark side, eagle of heaven.

Even the sun in heaven can be curbed and chastened at last
By the life in the hearts of men.
And you, great bird, sun-starer, heavy black beak
Can be put out of office as sacrifice bringer.

D. H. LAWRENCE

On a Peacock

I

Thou foolish Bird, of Feathers proud,
Whose Lustre yet thine Eyes ne're see:
The gazing Wonder of the Crowd,
Beauteous, not to thy self, but Me!
Thy Hellish Voice doth those affright,
Whose Eyes were charmed at thy sight.

II

Vainly thou think'st, those Eyes of thine
Were such as sleepy *Argus* lost;
When he was touch'd with rod Divine,
Who lat of Vigilance did boast.
Little at best they'll thee avail,
Not in thine *Head*, but in thy *Tayl*.

III

Wiseman do *forward* look to try
What will in *following* Moments come:
Backward thy useless Eyes do ly,
Nor do enquire of *future* doom.
'Nothing can remedy what's past;
Wisdom must guard the present cast.'

[29]

IV

Our Eyes are best employ'd at home,
Not when they are on others plac'd:
From thine but little good can come,
Which never on thy self are cast:
What can of such a Tool be made:
A Tayl *well-furnish'd*, but an empty Head.

THOMAS HEYRICK

The Landrail

How sweet and pleasant grows the way
Through summer time again
While Landrails call from day to day
Amid the grass and grain

We hear it in the weeding time
When knee deep waves the corn
We hear it in the summers prime
Through meadows night and morn

And now I hear it in the grass
That grows as sweet again
And let a minutes notice pass
And now tis in the grain

Tis like a fancy every where
A sort of living doubt
We know tis somthing but it neer
Will blab the secret out

If heard in close or meadow plots
It flies if we pursue
But follows if we notice not
The close and meadow through

Boys know the note of many a bird
In their birdnesting bounds
But when the landrails noise is heard
They wonder at the sounds

They look in every tuft of grass
Thats in their rambles met
They peep in every bush they pass
And none the wiser get

And still they hear the craiking sound
And still they wonder why
It surely cant be under ground
Nor is it in the sky

And yet tis heard in every vale
An undiscovered song
And makes a pleasant wonder tale
For all the summer long

The shepherd whistles through his hands
And starts with many a whoop
His busy dog across the lands
In hopes to fright it up

Tis still a minutes length or more
Till dogs are off and gone
Then sings and louder then before
But keeps the secret on

Yet accident will often meet
The nest within its way
And weeders when they weed the wheat
Discover where they lay

And mowers on the meadow lea
Chance on their noisey guest
And wonder what the bird can be
That lays without a nest

BIRDS

In simple holes that birds will rake
When dusting on the ground
They drop their eggs of curious make
Deep blotched and nearly round

A mystery still to men and boys
Who know not where they lay
And guess it but a summer noise
Among the meadow hay

JOHN CLARE

To the Man-of-War Bird

Thou who hast slept all night upon the storm,
Waking renew'd on thy prodigious pinions,
(Burst the wild storm? above it thou ascended'st,

And rested on the sky, thy slave that cradled thee),
Now a blue point, far, far in heaven floating,
As to the light emerging here on deck I watch thee,
(Myself a speck, a point on the world's floating vast).

Far, far at sea,
After the night's fierce drifts have strewn the shore with wrecks,
With re-appearing day as now so happy and serene,
The rosy and elastic dawn, the flashing sun,
The limpid spread of air cerulean,
Thou also re-appearest.

Thou born to match the gale (thou art all wings),
To cope with heaven and earth and sea and hurricane,
Thou ship of air that never furl'st thy sails
Days, even weeks untired and onward, through spaces, realms
  gyrating,

At dusk that look'st on Senegal, at morn America,
That sport'st amid the lightning-flash and thunder-cloud,
In them, in thy experiences, had'st thou my soul,
What joys! what joys were thine!

WALT WHITMAN

The Curlew

Sweet-throated cry, by one no longer heard
Who, more than many, loved the wandering bird,
Unchanged through generations and renewed,
Perpetual child of its own solitude,
The same on rocks and over sea I hear
Return now with his unreturning year.
How softly now it flies across the sands,
Image of change unchanging, changing lands
From year to year, yet always found near home
Where waves in sunlight break in restless foam.
Old though the cave is, this outlives the cave.
And the grey pool that shuddered when it gave
The landscape life, reveals where time has grown,
Turning green, slowly forming tears to stone.
The quick light of that cry disturbs the gloom.
It passes now, and rising from its tomb,
Carries remorse across the sea where I
Wait on the shore, still listening to that cry
Which bears a ghostly listening to my own;
Such life is hidden in the ringing stone
That rests, unmatched by any natural thing,
And joins, unheard, the wave-crest and the wing.

VERNON WATKINS

To the Snipe

Lover of swamps
And quagmire overgrown
With hassock-tufts of sedge, where fear encamps
Around thy home alone,

The trembling grass
Quakes from the human foot,
Nor bears the weight of man to let him pass
Where thou, alone and mute,

Sittest at rest
In safety, near the clump
Of huge flag-forest that thy haunts invest
Or some old sallow stump,

Thriving on seams
That tiny islands swell,
Just hilling from the mud and rancid streams,
Suiting thy nature well;

For here thy bill,
Suited by wisdom good,
Of rude unseemly length, doth delve and drill
The jellied mass for food;

And here, mayhap,
When summer suns have drest
The moor's rude, desolate and spongy lap,
May hide thy mystic nest —

Mystic indeed;
For isles that oceans make
Are scarcely more secure for birds to build
Than this flag-hidden lake.

Boys thread the woods
To their remotest shades;
But in these marshy flats, these stagnant floods,
Security pervades.

[34]

From year to year
Places untrodden lie,
Where man nor boy nor stock hath ventured near,
Naught gazed on but the sky

And fowl that dread
The very breath of man,
Hiding in spots that never knew his tread,
A wild and timid clan,

Widgeon and teal
And wild duck — restless lot,
That from man's dreaded sight will ever steal
To the most dreary spot.

Here tempests howl
Around each flaggy plot,
Where they who dread man's sight, the water fowl,
Hide and are frightened not.

'Tis power divine
That heartens them to brave
The roughest tempest and at ease recline
On marshes or the wave.

Yet instinct knows
Not safety's bounds: — to shun
The firmer ground where skulking fowler goes
With searching dogs and gun,

By tepid springs
Scarcely one stride across
(Through bramble from its edge a shelter flings
Thy safety is at loss)

— And never choose
The little sinky foss,
Streaking the moors whence spa-red water spews
From pudges fringed with moss;

Freebooters there,
Intent to kill or slay,
Startle with cracking guns the trepid air,
And dogs thy haunts betray.

From danger's reach
Here thou art safe to roam,
Far as these washy flag-sown marshes stretch
A still and quiet home.

In these thy haunts
I've gleaned habitual love;
From the vague world where pride and folly taunts
I muse and look above.

Thy solitudes
The unbounded heaven esteems,
And here my heart warms into higher moods
And dignifying dreams.

I see the sky
Smile on the meanest spot,
Giving to all that creep or walk or fly
A calm and cordial lot.

Thine teaches me
Right feelings to employ —
That in the dreariest places peace will be
A dweller and a joy.

JOHN CLARE

'O lapwing, thou fliest around the heath'

O lapwing, thou fliest around the heath,
Nor seest the net that is spread beneath.
Why dost thou not fly among the corn fields?
They cannot spread nets where a harvest yields.

WILLIAM BLAKE

Common Terns

Quiet as conscience on the Stock Exchange
I crept across a gradient of shelving shingle
To where in a gravel-working water lay
Brackish and thick with weed, slate-blue and viscous.

Out on a spit were common terns in hundreds:
Terns with their delicate staggered swallow-wings
And striding lilting flight and hovering flutter
Like kestrels into the wind, and sheer stoop
Straight for the darting goby in the pool.

And as I rose above the shingle crest
They burst into the air like an explosion,
A white gusher, a quarter-mile-high fountain
Mushrooming out into fragments, yet each perfect,
A column of shrieking milling sound-at-pressure,
Terribly like man's work — as if they were
An atomic bomb and I some engineer.

I felt my human agony then to the full,
That I for simile of that natural vision
Should so conclusively immediately choose
Utter destruction absolute desolation;
And sat there numb and grievous, ashamed to move,
As wildly they whirled and wheeled and slowly settled,
Bright sediment down the blue glass of air.

PATRIC DICKINSON

[37]

Of the Cuckoo

Thou booby, say'st thou nothing but cuckoo?
The robin and the wren can thee outdo.
They to us play thoróugh their little throats,
Not one, but sundry pretty tuneful notes.

But thou hast fellows, some like thee can do
Little but suck our eggs, and sing cuckoo.

Thy notes do not first welcome in our spring,
Not dost thou its first tokens to us bring.
Birds less than thee by far, like prophets, do
Tell us 'tis coming, though not by cuckoo.

Nor dost thou summer have away with thee,
Though thou a yawling, bawling cuckoo be.
When thou dost cease among us to appear,
Then doth our harvest bravely crown our year.

But thou hast fellows, some like thee can do
Little but suck our eggs, and sing cuckoo.

Since cuckoos forward not our early spring,
Nor help with notes to bring our harvest in:

And since while here she only makes a noise,
So pleasing unto none as girls and boys,
The formalist we may compare her to,
For he doth suck our eggs, and sing cuckoo.

JOHN BUNYAN

To the Cuckoo

O blithe New-comer! I have heard,
I hear thee and rejoice,
O Cuckoo! shall I call thee Bird,
Or but a wandering Voice?

While I am lying on the grass
Thy twofold shout I hear,
From hill to hill it seems to pass,
At once far off, and near.

Though babbling only to the Vale,
Of sunshine and of flowers,
Thou bringest unto me a tale
Of visionary hours.

Thrice welcome, darling of the Spring!
Even yet thou art to me
No bird, but an invisible thing,
A voice, a mystery;

The same whom in my school-boy days
I listened to; that Cry
Which made me look a thousand ways
In bush, and tree, and sky.

To seek thee did I often rove
Through woods and on the green;
And thou wert still a hope, a love;
Still longed for, never seen.

And I can listen to thee yet;
Can lie upon the plain
And listen, till I do beget
That golden time again.

O blessèd Bird! the earth we pace
Again appears to be
An unsubstantial, faery place;
That is fit home for Thee!

WILLIAM WORDSWORTH

The Cuckoo

The cuckoo, like a hawk in flight,
With narrow pointed wings
Whews o'er our heads — soon out of sight
And as she flies she sings:
And darting down the hedgerow side
She scares the little bird
Who leaves the nest it cannot hide
While plaintive notes are heard.

I've watched it on an old oak tree
Sing half an hour away
Until its quick eye noticed me
And then it whewed away.
Its mouth when open shone as red
As hips upon the brier,
Like stock doves seemed its winged head
But striving to get higher

It heard me rustle and above leaves
Soon did its flight pursue,
Still waking summer's melodies
And singing as it flew.
So quick it flies from wood to wood
'Tis miles off 'ere you think it gone;
I've thought when I have listening stood
Full twenty sang — when only one.

When summer from the forest starts
Its melody with silence lies,
And, like a bird from foreign parts,
It cannot sing for all it tries.
'Cuck cuck' it cries and mocking boys
Crie 'Cuck' and then it stutters more
Till quick forgot its own sweet voice
It seems to know itself no more.

JOHN CLARE

[40]

The Nightjar

We loved our Nightjar, but she would not stay with us.
We had found her lying as dead, but soft and warm,
Under the apple tree beside the old thatched wall.
Two days we kept her in a basket by the fire,
Fed her, and thought she well might live — till suddenly
In the very moment of most confiding hope
She raised herself all tense, quivered and drooped and died.
Tears sprang into my eyes — why not? the heart of man
Soon sets itself to love a living companion,
The more so if by chance it asks some care of him.
And this one had the kind of loveliness that goes
Far deeper than the optic nerve — full fathom five
To the soul's ocean cave, where Wonder and Reason
Tell their alternate dreams of how the world was made.
So wonderful she was — her wings the wings of night
But powdered here and there with tiny golden clouds
And wave-line markings like sea-ripples on the sand.
O how I wish I might never forget that bird —
Never!
         But even now, like all beauty of earth,
She is fading from me into the dusk of Time.

SIR HENRY NEWBOLT

Humming-bird

I can imagine, in some otherworld
Primeval-dumb, far back
In that most awful stillness, that only gasped and hummed,
Humming-birds raced down the avenues.

Before anything had a soul,
While life was a heave of Matter, half inanimate,
This little bit chipped off in brilliance
And went whizzing through the slow, vast, succulent stems.

I believe there were no flowers then,
In the world where the humming-bird flashed ahead of creation.
I believed he pierced the slow vegetable veins with his long beak.

Probably he was big
As mosses, and little lizards, they say, were once big.
Probably he was a jabbing, terrifying monster.

We look at him through the wrong end of the long telescope
    of Time,
Luckily for us.

D. H. LAWRENCE

The Skylark

Bird of the wilderness,
Blithesome and cumberless,
Sweet be thy matin o'er moorland and lea!
Emblem of happiness,
Blest is thy dwelling-place —
O to abide in the desert with thee!
Wild is thy lay and loud,
Far in the downy cloud,
Love gives it energy, love gave it birth.
Where, on thy dewy wing,
Where art thou journeying?
Thy lay is in heaven, thy love is on earth.

O'er fell and mountain sheen,
O'er moor and mountain green,
O'er the red streamer that heralds the day,
Over the cloudlet dim,
Over the rainbow's rim,
Musical cherub, soar, singing, away!
Then, when the gloaming comes,
Low in the heather blooms

Sweet will thy welcome and bed of love be!
  Emblem of happiness,
   Blest is thy dwelling-place —
O to abide in the desert with thee!

JAMES HOGG

To a Skylark

Ethereal minstrel! pilgrim of the sky!
Dost thou despise the earth where cares abound?
Or, while the wings aspire, are heart and eye
Both with thy nest upon the dewy ground?
Thy nest which thou canst drop into at will,
Those quivering wings composed, that music still!

Leave to the nightingale her shady wood;
A privacy of glorious light is thine;
Whence thou dost pour upon the world a flood
Of harmony, with instinct more divine;
Type of the wise who soar, but never roam;
True to the kindred points of Heaven and Home!

WILLIAM WORDSWORTH

To a Skylark

  Hail to thee, blithe Spirit!
   Bird thou never wert,
That from Heaven, or near it,
  Pourest thy full heart
In profuse strains of unpremeditated art.

[43]

Higher still and higher
    From the earth thou springest
Like a cloud of fire;
    The blue deep thou wingest,
And singing still dost soar, and soaring ever singest.

In the golden lightning
    Of the sunken sun,
O'er which clouds are bright'ning,
    Thou dost float and run;
Like an unbodied joy whose race is just begun.

The pale purple even
    Melts around thy flight;
Like a star of Heaven,
    In the broad daylight
Thou art unseen, but yet I hear thy shrill delight,

Keen as are the arrows
    Of that silver sphere,
Whose intense lamp narrows
    In the white dawn clear
Until we hardly see — we feel that it is there.

All the earth and air
    With thy voice is loud,
As, when night is bare,
    From one lonely cloud
The moon rains out her beams, and Heaven is overflowed.

What thou art we know not;
    What is most like thee?
From rainbow clouds there flow not
    Drops so bright to see
As from thy presence showers a rain of melody.

Like a Poet hidden
    In the light of thought,
Singing hymns unbidden.
    Till the world is wrought
To sympathy with hopes and fears it heeded not:

[44]

Like a high-born maiden
  In a palace-tower,
Soothing her love-laden
  Soul in secret hour
With music sweet as love, which overflows her bower:

Like a glow-worm golden
  In a dell of dew,
Scattering unbeholden
  Its aëreal hue
Among the flowers and grass, which screen it from the view!

Like a rose embowered
  In its own green leaves,
By warm winds deflowered,
  Till the scent it gives
Makes faint with too much sweet those heavy-wingèd thieves:

Sound of vernal showers
  On the twinkling grass,
Rain-awakened flowers,
  All that ever was
Joyous, and clear, and fresh, thy music doth surpass:

Teach us, Sprite or Bird,
  What sweet thoughts are thine:
I have never heard
  Praise of love or wine
That painted forth a flood of rapture so divine.

Chorus Hymeneal,
  Or triumphal chant,
Matched with thine would be all
  But an empty vaunt,
A thing wherein we feel there is some hidden want.

What objects are the fountains
  Of thy happy strain?
What fields, or waves, or mountains?
  What shapes of sky or plain?
What love of thine own kind? what ignorance of pain?

[45]

With thy clear keen joyance
    Languor cannot be:
Shadow of annoyance
    Never came near thee:
Thou lovest — but ne'er knew love's sad satiety.

Waking or asleep,
    Thou of death must deem
Things more true and deep
    Than we mortals dream,
Or how could thy notes flow in such a crystal stream?

We look before and after,
    And pine for what is not:
Our sincerest laughter
    With some pain is fraught;
Our sweetest songs are those that tell of saddest thought.

Yet if we could scorn
    Hate, and pride, and fear;
If we were things born
    Not to shed a tear,
I know not how thy joy we ever should come near.

Better than all measures
    Of delightful sound,
Better than all treasures
    That in books are found,
Thy skill to poet were, thou scorner of the ground!

Teach me half the gladness
    That thy brain must know,
Such harmonious madness
    From my lips would flow
The world should listen then — as I am listening now.

PERCY BYSSHE SHELLEY

[46]

Shelley's Skylark

(*The neighbourhood of Leghorn: March 1887*)

Somewhere afield here something lies
In Earth's oblivious eyeless trust
That moved a poet to prophecies —
A pinch of unseen, unguarded dust:

The dust of the lark that Shelley heard,
And made immortal through times to be: —
Though it only lived like another bird,
And knew not its immortality:

Lived its meek life; then, one day, fell —
A little ball of feather and bone;
And how it perished, when piped farewell,
And where it wastes, are alike unknown.

Maybe it rests in the loam I view,
Maybe it throbs in a myrtle's green,
Maybe it sleeps in the coming hue
Of a grape on the slopes of yon inland scene.

Go find it, faeries, go and find
That tiny pinch of priceless dust,
And bring a casket silver-lined,
And framed of gold that gems encrust;

And we will lay it safe therein,
And consecrate it to endless time;
For it inspired a bard to win
Ecstatic heights in thought and rhyme.

THOMAS HARDY

[47]

The Lark Ascending

He rises and begins to round,
He drops the silver chain of sound,
Of many links without a break,
In chirrup, whistle, slur and shake,
All intervolved and spreading wide,
Like water-dimples down a tide
Where ripple ripple overcurls
And eddy into eddy whirls;
A press of hurried notes that run
So fleet they scarce are more than one,
Yet changeingly the trills repeat
And linger ringing while they fleet,
Sweet to the quick o' the ear, and dear
To her beyond the handmaid ear,
Who sits beside our inner springs,
Too often dry for this he brings,
Which seems the very jet of earth
At sight of sun, her music's mirth,
As up he wings the spiral stair,
A song of light, and pierces air
With fountain ardour, fountain play,
To reach the shining tops of day,
And drink in everything discerned
An ecstasy to music turned,
Impelled by what his happy bill
Disperses; drinking, showering still,
Unthinking save that he may give
His voice the outlet, there to live
Renewed in endless notes of glee,
So thirsty of his voice is he,
For all to hear and all to know
That he is joy, awake, aglow,
The tumult of the heart to hear
Through pureness filtered crystal-clear,
And know the pleasure sprinkled bright
By simple singing of delight,
Shrill, irreflective, unrestrained,

Rapt, ringing, on the jet sustained
Without a break, without a fall,
Sweet-silvery, sheer lyrical,
Perennial, quavering up the chord
Like myriad dews of sunny sward
That trembling into fulness shine,
And sparkle dropping argentine;
Such wooing as the ear receives
From zephyr caught in choric leaves
Of aspens when their chattering net
Is flushed to white with shivers wet;
And such the water-spirit's chime
On mountain heights in morning's prime,
Too freshly sweet to seem excess,
Too animate to need a stress;
But wider over many heads
The starry voice ascending spreads,
Awakening, as it waxes thin,
The best in us to him akin;
And every face to watch him raised
Puts on the light of children praised,
So rich our human pleasure ripes
When sweetness on sincereness pipes,
Though nought be promised from the seas,
But only a soft-ruffling breeze
Sweep glittering on a still content,
Serenity in ravishment.
For singing till his heaven fills,
'Tis love of earth that he instils,
And ever winging up and up,
Our valley is his golden cup,
And he the wine which overflows
To lift us with him as he goes;
The woods and brooks, the sheep and kine;
He is, the hills, the human line,
The meadows green, the fallows brown,
The dreams of labour in the town;
He sings the sap, the quickened veins;
The wedding song of sun and rains
He is, the dance of children, thanks

Of sowers, shout of primrose-banks,
And eye of violets while they breathe;
All these the circling song will wreathe,
And you shall hear the herb and tree,
The better heart of men shall see,
Shall feel celestially, as long
As you crave nothing save the song.

Was never voice of ours could say
Our inmost in the sweetest way,
Like yonder voice aloft, and link
All hearers in the song they drink.
Our wisdom speaks from failing blood,
Our passion is too full in flood,
We want the key of his wild note
Of truthful in a tuneful throat,
The song seraphically free
Of taint of personality,
So pure that it salutes the suns,
The voice of one for millions,
In whom the millions rejoice
For giving their one spirit voice.
Yet men have we, whom we revere,
Now names, and men still housing here,
Whose lives, by many a battle-dint
Defaced, and grinding wheels on flint,
Yield substance, though they sing not, sweet
For song our highest heaven to greet:
Whom heavenly singing gives us new,
Enspheres them brilliant in our blue,
From firmest base to farthest leap,
Because their love of Earth is deep,
And they are warriors in accord
With life to serve, and pass reward,
So touching purest and so heard
In the brain's reflex of yon bird:
Wherefore their soul in me, or mine,
Through self-forgetfulness divine,
In them, that song aloft maintains,
To fill the sky and thrill the plains

With showerings drawn from human stores,
As he to silence nearer soars,
Extends the world at wings and dome,
More spacious making more our home,
Till lost on his aërial rings
In light, and then the fancy sings.

GEORGE MEREDITH

The Swallow

Foolish prater, what dost thou
So early at my window do
With thy tuneless serenade?
Well't had been had Tereus made
Thee as dumb as Philomel;
There his knife had done but well.
In thy undiscovered nest,
Thou dost all the winter rest,
And dreamest o'er thy summer joys,
Free from the stormy seasons's noise,
Free from th'ill thou'st done to me:
Who disturbs, or seeks out thee?
Hadst thou all the charming notes
Of the wood's poetic throats,
All thy art could never pay
What thou'st ta'en from me away.
Cruel bird, thou'st ta'en away
A dream out of my arms today,
A dream that ne'er must equalled be
By all that waking eyes may see.
Thou this damage to repair,
Nothing half so sweet or fair,
Nothing half so good canst bring,
Though men say thou bring'st the spring.

ABRAHAM COWLEY

The Faithful Swallow

When summer shone
Its sweetest on
An August day,
"Here evermore,"
I said, "I'll stay;
Not go away
To another shore
As fickle they!"

December came:
'Twas not the same!
I did not know
Fidelity
Would serve me so.
Frost, hunger, snow;
And now, ah me,
Too late to go!

THOMAS HARDY

A Swallow

Has slipped through a fracture in the snow-sheet
Which is still our sky —

She flicks past, ahead of her name,
Twinkling away out over the lake.

Reaching this way and that way, with her scissors,
Snipping midges
Trout are still too numb and sunken to stir for.

Sahara clay ovens, at mirage heat,
Glazed her blues, and still she is hot.

She wearied of snatching clegs off the lugs of buffaloes
And of lassooing the flirt-flags of gazelles.

They told her the North was one giant snowball
Rolling South. She did not believe them.
So she exchanged the starry chart of Columbus
For a beggar's bowl of mud.

Setting her compass-tremor tail-needles
She harpooned a wind
That wallowed in the ocean,
Working her barbs deeper
Through that twisting mass she came —

Did she close her eyes and trust in God?
No, she saw lighthouses
Streaming in chaos
Like sparks from a chimney —

She had fixed her instruments on home.

And now, suddenly, into a blanch-tree stillness
A silence of celandines,
A fringing and stupor of frost
She bursts, weightless —
                                        to anchor
On eggs frail as frost.

There she goes, flung taut on her leash,
Her eyes at her mouth-corners,
Water-skiing out across a wind
That wrecks great flakes against windscreens.

                                        TED HUGHES

[53]

Sedge-warblers

This beauty made me dream there was a time
Long past and irrecoverable, a clime
Where any brook so radiant racing clear
Through buttercup and kingcup bright as brass
But gentle, nourishing the meadow grass
That leans and scurries in the wind, would bear
Another beauty, divine and feminine,
Child to the sun, a nymph whose soul unstained
Could love all day, and never hate or tire,
A lover of mortal or immortal kin.
And yet, rid of this dream, ere I had drained
Its poison, quieted was my desire
So that I only looked into the water,
Clearer than any goddess or man's daughter,
And hearkened while it combed the dark green hair
And shook the millions of the blossoms white
Of water-crowfoot, and curdled to one sheet
The flowers fallen from the chestnuts in the park
Far off. And sedge-warblers, clinging so light
To willow twigs, sang longer than the lark,
Quick, shrill, or grating, a song to match the heat
Of the strong sun, nor less the water's cool,
Gushing through narrows, swirling in the pool.
Their song that lacks all words, all melody,
All sweetness almost, was dearer then to me
Than sweetest voice that sings in tune sweet words.
This was the best of May — the small brown birds
Wisely reiterating endlessly
What no man learnt yet, in or out of school.

EDWARD THOMAS

An Epitaph on a Robin Redbreast

Tread lightly here, for here, 'tis said,
When piping winds are hushed around,
A small note wakes from underground
Where now his tiny bones are laid.
No more in lone and leafless groves,
With ruffled wing and faded breast,
His friendless, homeless spirit roves —
Gone to the world where birds are blest!
Where never cat glides o'er the green,
Or schoolboy's giant form is seen;
But love, and joy and smiling spring
Inspire their little souls to sing!

SAMUEL ROGERS

The Robin

When up aloft
I fly and fly,
I see in pools
The shining sky,
And a happy bird
Am I, am I!

When I descend
Towards their brink
I stand, and look,
And stoop, and drink,
And bathe my wings,
And chink and prink.

When winter frost
Makes earth as steel
I search and search

But find no meal,
And most unhappy
Then I feel.

But when it lasts,
And snows still fall,
I get to feel
No grief at all,
For I turn to a cold stiff
Feathery ball!

THOMAS HARDY

The Yellow-hammer

When, towards the summer's close,
  Lanes are dry,
And unclipt the hedgethorn rows,
  There we fly!

While the harvest waggons pass
  With their load,
Shedding corn upon the grass
  By the road.

In a flock we follow them,
  On and on,
Seize a wheat-ear by the stem,
  And are gone. . . .

With our funny little song,
  Thus you may
Often see us flit along,
  Day by day.

THOMAS HARDY

[56]

The Nightingale

As it fell upon a day
In the merry month of May,
Sitting in a pleasant shade
Which a grove of myrtles made,
Beasts did leap and birds did sing,
Trees did grow and plants did spring;
Every thing did banish moan
Save the Nightingale alone.
She, poor bird, as all forlorn,
Lean'd her breast up-till a thorn,
And there sung the dolefull'st ditty,
That to hear it was great pity.

'Fie, fie, fie!', now would she cry;
'Tereu, tereu!', by and by:
That to hear her so complain
Scarce I could from tears refrain;
For her griefs so lively shown
Made me think upon mine own.
— Ah, thought I, thou mourn'st in vain,
None takes pity on thy pain:
Senseless trees, they cannot hear thee,
Ruthless beasts, they will not cheer thee;
King Pandion, he is dead,
All thy friends are lapp'd in lead:
All thy fellow birds do sing
Careless of thy sorrowing:
Even so, poor bird, like thee
None alive will pity me.

RICHARD BARNFIELD

To a Nightingale

Sweet Bird, that sing'st away the early Howres,
Of Winters past or coming void of Care,
Well pleased with Delights which Present are,
Faire Seasones, budding Sprayes, sweet-smelling Flowers:
To Rocks, to Springs, to Rills, from leavy Bowres
Thou thy Creators Goodnesse dost declare,
And what deare Gifts on thee hee did not spare,
A Staine to humane sense in sinne that lowres.
What Soule can be so sicke, which by thy Songs
(Attir'd in sweetnesse) sweetly is not driven
Quite to forget Earths turmoiles, spights, and wrongs,
And lift a reverend Eye and Thought to Heaven?
    Sweet Artlesse Songstarre, thou my Minde dost raise
    To Ayres of Spheares, yes, and to Angels Layes.

WILLIAM DRUMMOND

'The nightingale, as soon as April bringeth'

The nightingale, as soon as April bringeth
Unto her rested sense a perfect waking,
While late bare earth, proud of new clothing, springeth,
Sings out her woes, a thorn her song book making;
   And mournfully bewailing,
   Her throat in tunes expresseth
   What grief her breast oppresseth,
   For Tereus' force on her chaste will prevailing.
     O Philomela fair, O take some gladness,
     That here is juster cause of plaintful sadness:
     Thine earth now springs, mine fadeth,
     Thy thorn without, my thorn my heart invadeth.

Alas, she hath no other cause of anguish
But Tereus' love, on her by strong hand wroken,
Wherein she suff'ring all her spirits' languish,
Full womanlike complains her will was broken.
   But I, who, daily craving,
   Cannot have to content me,
   Have more cause to lament me,
   Since wanting is more woe than too much having.
     O Philomela fair, O take some gladness,
     That here is juster cause of plaintful sadness:
     Thine earth now springs, mine fadeth,
     Thy thorn without, my thorn my heart invadeth.

SIR PHILIP SIDNEY

Ode: To the Nightingale

O thou that to the moonlight vale
Warblest oft thy plaintive tale,
What time the village murmurs cease,
And the still eve is hushed to peace,
When now no busy sound is heard,
Contemplation's favourite bird!

Chantress of night, whose amorous song
(First heard the tufted groves among)
Warns wanton Mabba to begin
Her revels on the circled green,
Whene'er by meditation led,
I nightly seek some distant mead,

A short repose of cares to find,
And soothe my love-distracted mind,
O fail not then, sweet Philomel,
Thy sadly warbled woes to tell;
In sympathetic numbers join
Thy pangs of luckless love with mine!

So may no swain's rude hand infest
Thy tender young, and rob thy nest;
Nor ruthless fowler's guileful snare
Lure thee to leave the fields of air,
No more to visit vale or shade,
Some barbarous virgin's captive made.

JOSEPH WARTON

The Nightingale and
the Glowworm

A nightingale, that all day long
Had cheered the village with his song,
Nor yet at eve his note suspended,
Nor yet when eventide was ended,
Began to feel, as well he might,
The keen demands of appetite;
When, looking eagerly around,
He spied far off, upon the ground,
A something shining in the dark,
And knew the glowworm by his spark;
So, stooping down from hawthorn top,
He thought to put him in his crop.
The worm, aware of his intent,
Harangued him thus, right eloquent —
    Did you admire my lamp, quoth he,
As much as I your minstrelsy,
You would abhor to do me wrong,
As much as I to spoil your song;
For 'twas the self-same pow'r divine
Taught you to sing, and me to shine;
That you with music, I with light,
Might beautify and cheer the night.
    The songster heard his short oration,
And, warbling out his approbation,
Released him, as my story tells,
And found a supper somewhere else.
    Hence jarring sectaries may learn
Their real int'rest to discern;
That brother should not war with brother,
And worry and devour each other;
But sing and shine by sweet consent,
Till life's poor transient night is spent,
Respecting in each other's case
The gifts of nature and of grace.

Those Christians best deserve the name
Who studiously make peace their aim;
Peace, both the duty and the prize
Of him that creeps and him that flies.

WILLIAM COWPER

Ode to a Nightingale

My heart aches, and a drowsy numbness pains
  My sense, as though of hemlock I had drunk,
Or emptied some dull opiate to the drains
  One minute past, and Lethe-wards had sunk:
'Tis not through envy of thy happy lot,
  But being too happy in thy happiness, —
    That thou, light-winged Dryad of the trees,
      In some melodious plot
  Of beechen green, and shadows numberless,
    Singest of summer in full-throated ease.

O for a draught of vintage, that hath been
  Cool'd a long age in the deep-delved earth,
Tasting of Flora and the country-green,
  Dance, and Provençal song, and sun-burnt mirth!
O for a beaker full of the warm South,
  Full of the true, the blushful Hippocrene,
    With beaded bubbles winking at the brim,
      And purple-stained mouth;
  That I might drink, and leave the world unseen,
    And with thee fade away into the forest dim:

Fade far away, dissolve, and quite forget
  What thou among the leaves hast never known,
The weariness, the fever, and the fret
  Here, where men sit and hear each other groan;

Where palsy shakes a few, sad, last gray hairs,
 Where youth grows pale, and spectre-thin, and dies;
  Where but to think is to be full of sorrow
   And leaden-eyed despairs;
 Where beauty cannot keep her lustrous eyes,
  Or new Love pine at them beyond to-morrow.

Away! away! for I will fly to thee,
 Not charioted by Bacchus and his pards,
But on the viewless wings of Poesy,
 Though the dull brain perplexes and retards:
Already with thee! tender is the night,
 And haply the Queen-Moon is on her throne,
  Cluster'd around by all her starry Fays;
   But here there is no light,
 Save what from heaven is with the breezes blown
  Through verdurous glooms and winding mossy ways.

I cannot see what flowers are at my feet,
 Nor what soft incense hangs upon the boughs,
But, in embalmed darkness, guess each sweet
 Wherewith the seasonable month endows
The grass, the thicket, and the fruit-tree wild;
 White hawthorn, and the pastoral eglantine;
  Fast-fading violets cover'd up in leaves;
   And mid-May's eldest child,
 The coming musk-rose, full of dewy wine,
  The murmurous haunt of flies on summer eves.

Darkling I listen; and for many a time
 I have been half in love with easeful Death,
Call'd him soft names in many a mused rhyme,
 To take into the air my quiet breath;
Now more than ever seems it rich to die,
 To cease upon the midnight with no pain,
  While thou art pouring forth thy soul abroad
   In such an ecstasy!
 Still wouldst thou sing, and I have ears in vain
  To thy high requiem become a sod.

[63]

Thou wast not born for death, immortal Bird!
  No hungry generations tread thee down;
The voice I hear this passing night was heard
  In ancient days by emperor and clown:
Perhaps the self-same song that found a path
    Through the sad heart of Ruth, when sick for home,
      She stood in tears amid the alien corn;
        The same that oft-times hath
    Charm'd magic casements, opening on the foam
      Of perilous seas, in faery lands forlorn.

Forlorn! the very word is like a bell
  To toll me back from thee to my sole self!
Adieu! the fancy cannot cheat so well
  As she is famed to do, deceiving elf.
Adieu! adieu! thy plaintive anthem fades
  Past the near meadows, over the still stream,
    Up the hill-side; and now 'tis buried deep
      In the next valley-glades:
  Was it a vision, or a waking dream?
    Fled is that music: — do I wake or sleep?

JOHN KEATS

The Nightingale's Nest

Up this green woodland-ride let's softly rove,
And list the nightingale — she dwells just here.
Hush! let the wood-gate softly clap, for fear
The noise might drive her from her home of love;
For here I've heard her many a merry year —
At morn, at eve, nay, all the livelong day,
As though she lived on song. This very spot,
Just where that old man's beard all wildly trails
Rude arbours o'er the road and stops the way —

And where that child its bluebell flowers hath got,
Laughing and creeping through the mossy rails —
There have I hunted like a very boy,
Creeping on hands and knees through matted thorn
To find her nest and see her feed her young.
And vainly did I many hours employ:
All seemed as hidden as a thought unborn.
And where those crimping fern-leaves ramp among
The hazel's under-boughs, I've nestled down
And watched her while she sung; and her renown
Hath made me marvel that so famed a bird
Should have no better dress than russet brown.
Her wings would tremble in her ecstasy,
And feathers stand on end, as 'twere with joy,
And mouth wide open to release her heart
Of its out-sobbing songs. The happiest part
Of summer's fame she shared, for so to me
Did happy fancies shapen her employ;
But if I touched a bush or scarcely stirred,
All in a moment stopt. I watched in vain:
The timid bird had left the hazel bush,
And at a distance hid to sing again.
Lost in wilderness of listening leaves,
Rich ecstasy would pour its luscious strain,
Till envy spurred the emulating thrush
To start less wild and scarce inferior songs;
For while of half the year care him bereaves,
To damp the ardour of his speckled breast,
The nightingale to summer's life belongs,
And naked trees and winter's nipping wrongs
Are strangers to her music and her rest.
Her joys are evergreen, her world is wide —
Hark! there she is as usual — let's be hush —
For in this blackthorn-clump, if rightly guessed,
Her curious house is hidden. Part aside
These hazel branches in a gentle way
And stoop right cautious 'neath the rustling boughs,
For we will have another search to-day
And hunt this fern-strewn thorn-clump round and round;
And where this reeded wood-grass idly bows,

[65]

We'll wade right through, it is a likely nook:
In such like spots and often on the ground,
They'll build, where rude boys never think to look.
Ay, as I live! her secret nest is here,
Upon this whitethorn stump! I've searched about
For hours in vain. There! put that bramble by —
Nay, trample on its branches and get near.
How subtle is the bird! she started out,
And raised a plaintive note of danger nigh,
Ere we were past the brambles; and now, near
Her nest, she sudden stops — as choking fear
That might betray her home. So even now
We'll leave it as we found it: safety's guard
Of pathless solitudes shall keep it still.
See there! she's sitting on the old oak bough,
Mute in her fears; our presence doth retard
Her joys, and doubt turns every rapture chill.
Sing on, sweet bird! may no worse hap befall
Thy visions than the fear that now deceives.
We will not plunder music of its dower,
Nor turn this spot of happiness to thrall;
For melody seems hid in every flower
That blossoms near thy home. These harebells all
Seem bowing with the beautiful in song;
And gaping cuckoo, with its spotted leaves,
Seems blushing with the singing it has heard.
How curious is the nest! no other bird
Uses such loose materials, or weaves
Its dwelling in such spots: dead oaken leaves
Are placed without and velvet moss within,
And little scraps of grass, and — scant and spare,
Of what seem scarce materials — down and hair;
For from men's haunts she nothing seems to win.
Yet nature is the builder, and contrives
Homes for her children's comfort even here,
Where solitude's disciples spend their lives
Unseen, save when a wanderer passes near
Who loves such pleasant places. Deep adown
The nest is made, a hermit's mossy cell.
Snug lie her curious eggs in number five,

Of deadened green, or rather olive-brown;
And the old prickly thorn-bush guards them well.
So here we'll leave them, still unknown to wrong,
As the old woodland's legacy of song.

JOHN CLARE

Philomela

Hark!, ah, the nightingale —
The tawny-throated!
Hark, from that moonlit cedar what a burst!
What triumph! hark! — what pain!

O wanderer from a Grecian shore,
Still, after many years, in distant lands,
Still nourishing in thy bewilder'd brain
That wild, unquench'd, deep-sunken, old-world pain —
Say, will it never heal?
And can this fragrant lawn
With its cool trees, and night,
And the sweet, tranquil Thames,
And moonshine, and the dew,
To thy rack'd heart and brain
Afford no balm?

Dost thou to-night behold,
Here, through the moonlight on this English grass,
The unfriendly palace in the Thracian wild?
Dost thou again peruse
With hot cheeks and sear'd eyes
The too clear web, and thy dumb sister's shame?
Dost thou once more assay
Thy flight, and feel come over thee,
Poor fugitive, the feathery change
Once more, and once more seem to make resound

[67]

With love and hate, triumph and agony,
Lone Daulis, and the high Cephissian vale?
Listen, Eugenia —
How thick the bursts come crowding through the leaves!
Again — thou hearest?
Eternal passion!
Eternal pain!

MATTHEW ARNOLD

Nightingales

Beautiful must be the mountains whence ye come,
And bright in the fruitful valleys the streams, wherefrom
      Ye learn your song:
Where are those starry woods? O might I wander there,
  Among the flowers, which in that heavenly air
      Bloom the year long!

Nay, barren are those mountains and spent the streams:
Our song is the voice of desire, that haunts our dreams,
      A throe of the heart,
Whose pining visions dim, forbidden hopes profound,
  No dying cadence nor long sigh can sound,
      For all our art.

Alone, aloud in the raptured ear of men
We pour our dark nocturnal secret; and then,
      As night is withdrawn
From these sweet-springing meads and bursting boughs of May,
  Dream, while the innumerable choir of day
      Welcome the dawn.

ROBERT BRIDGES

The Nightingale near the House

Here is the soundless cypress on the lawn:
It listens, listens. Taller trees beyond
Listen. The moon at the unruffled pond
Stares. And you sing, you sing.

That star-enchanted song falls through the air
From lawn to lawn down terraces of sound,
Darts in white arrows on the shadowed ground;
While all the night you sing.

My dreams are flowers to which you are a bee,
As all night long I listen, and my brain
Receives your song, then loses it again
In moonlight on the lawn.

Now is your voice a marble high and white,
Then like a mist on fields of paradise;
Now is a raging fire, then is like ice,
Then breaks, and it is dawn.

HAROLD MONRO

Out of the Cradle Endlessly Rocking

Out of the cradle endlessly rocking,
Out of the mocking-bird's throat, the musical shuttle,
Out of the Ninth-month midnight,
Over the sterile sands, and the fields beyond, where the child
    leaving his bed wander'd alone, bareheaded, barefoot,
Down from the shower'd halo,
Up from the mystic play of shadows twining and twisting as if they
    were alive,

[69]

Out from the patches of briers and blackberries,
From the memories of the bird that chanted to me,
From your memories, sad brother, from the fitful risings and
    fallings I heard,
From under that yellow half-moon late-risen and swollen as if
    with tears,
From those beginning notes of yearning and love there in the mist,
From the thousand responses of my heart never to cease,
From the myriad thence-arous'd words,
From the word stronger and more delicious than any,
From such as now they start the scene revisiting,
As a flock, twittering, rising, or overhead passing,
Borne hither, ere all eludes me, hurriedly,
A man, yet by these tears a little boy again,
Throwing myself on the sand, confronting the waves,
I, chanter of pains and joys, uniter of here and hereafter,
Taking all hints to use them, but swiftly leaping beyond them,
A reminiscence sing.

One Paumanok,
When the lilac-scent was in the air and Fifth-month grass was
    growing,
Up this seashore in some briers,
Two feather'd guests from Alabama, two together,
And their nest, and four light-green eggs spotted with brown,
And every day the he-bird to and fro near at hand,
And every day the she-bird crouch'd on her nest, silent, with
    bright eyes,
And every day I, curious boy, never too close, never disturbing
    them,
Cautiously peering, absorbing, translating.

Shine! shine! shine!
Pour down your warmth, great sun!
While we bask, we two together.

Two together!
Winds blow south, or winds blow north,
Day come white, or night come black,
Home, or rivers and mountains from home,

[70]

Singing all time, minding no time,
While we two keep together.

Till of a sudden,
May-be kill'd, unknown to her mate,
One forenoon the she-bird crouch'd not on the nest,
Nor return'd that afternoon, nor the next,
Nor ever appear'd again.

And thenceforward all summer in the sound of the sea,
And at night under the full of the moon in calmer weather,
Over the hoarse surging of the sea,
Or flitting from brier to brier by day,
I saw, I heard at intervals the remaining one, the he-bird,
The solitary guest from Alabama.

Blow! blow! blow!
Blow up sea-winds along Paumanok's shore;
I wait and I wait till you blow my mate to me.

Yes, when the stars glisten'd,
All night long on the prong of a moss-scallop'd stake,
Down almost amid the slapping waves,
Sat the lone singer wonderful causing tears.

He call'd on his mate,
He pour'd forth the meanings which I of all men know.

WALT WHITMAN

The Mocking-bird

A golden pallor of voluptuous light
Filled the warm southern night:
The moon, clear orbed, above the sylvan scene
Moved like a stately queen,
So rife with conscious beauty all the while,
What could she do but smile
At her own perfect loveliness below,
Glassed in the tranquil flow
Of crystal fountains and unruffled streams?
Half lost in waking dreams,
As down the loneliest forest dell I strayed,
Lo! from a neighboring glade,
Flashed through the drifts of moonshine, swiftly came
A fairy shape of flame.
It rose in dazzling spirals overhead,
Whence to wild sweetness wed,
Poured marvelous melodies, silvery trill on trill;
The very leaves grew still
On the charmed trees to hearken; while for me,
Heart-trilled to ecstasy,
I followed — followed the bright shape that flew,
Still circling up the blue,
Till as a fountain that has reached its height,
Falls back in sprays of light
Slowly dissolved, so that enrapturing lay
Divinely melts away
Through tremulous spaces to a music-mist,
Soon by the fitful breeze
    How gently kissed
Into remote and tender silences.

PAUL HAMILTON HAYNE

The Blackbird

The blackbird has a thousand whims
In choosing places for her nest
In spots that so unlikely seems
As want of skill and hardly taste
Upon the bindings of the hedge
On water grains of high oak tree
In roots o'er looked by kecks and sedge
On thorns where every eye may see.

And on a gatepost's very top
O'erhung with boughs will wonder stare
To find them — shepherds laughing stop
And think that boys have placed it there
On woodstacks in a cottage yard
Nay shelved upon an hovel stone
I've marked them with a strange regard
As nests some foreign birds might own.

My wonder I could scarce conceal
And what surprised me more than all
Between the spokes of an old wheel
That leaned against an hovel wall
Some moss was seen; I thought it laid
By boys to make each other stare
But bye and bye a nest was made
And eggs like fairy gifts were there.

JOHN CLARE

The Blackbird

Ov al the birds upon the wing
Between the zunny show'rs o' spring,
Var al the lark, a-swingèn high,
Míd zing sweet ditties to the sky,

[73]

An' sparrers, clust'ren roun' the bough,
Mid chatter to the men at plough;
The blackbird, hoppèn down along
The hedge, da zing the gâyest zong.

'Tis sweet, wi' yerly-wakèn eyes
To zee the zun when vust da rise,
Ar, hālen underwood an' lops
Vrom new-plēsh'd hedges ar vrom copse
To snatch oon's nammet down below
A tree wher primruosen da grow,
But ther's noo time the whol dā long
Lik' evemen wi' the blackbird's zong.

Var when my work is al a-done
Avore the zettèn o' the zun,
Then blushèn Jian da wā'k along
The hedge to mit me in the drong,
An' stây till al is dim an' dark
Bezides the ashen tree's white bark.
An' al bezides the blackbird's shrill
An' runnèn evemen-whissle's still.

How in my buoyhood I did rove
Wi' pryèn eyes along the drove,
Var blackbirds' nestes in the quick-
Set hedges high, an' green, an' thick;
Ar clim' al up, wi' clingèn knees,
Var crows' nestes in swayen trees,
While frighten'd blackbirds down below
Did chatter o' ther well-know'd foe.

An' we da hear the blackbirds zing
Ther sweetest ditties in the spring,
When nippèn win's na muore da blow
Vrom narthern skies wi' sleet ar snow,
But drēve light doust along between
The cluose leane-hedges, thick an' green;
An' zoo th' blackbird down along
The hedge da zing the gâyest zong.

WILLIAM BARNES

The Blackbird

O blackbird! sing me something well:
  While all the neighbours shoot thee round,
  I keep smooth plats of fruitful ground,
Where thou mayst warble, eat and dwell.

The espaliers and the standards all
  Are thine; the range of lawn and park:
  The unnetted black-hearts ripen dark,
All thine, against the garden wall.

Yet, though I spared thee all the spring,
  Thy sole delight is, sitting still,
  With that gold dagger of thy bill
To fret the summer jenneting.

A golden bill! the silver tongue,
  Cold February loved, is dry;
  Plenty corrupts the melody
That made thee famous once, when young:

And in the sultry garden-squares,
  Now thy flute-notes are changed to coarse,
  I hear thee not at all, or hoarse
As when a hawker hawks his wares.

Take warning! he that will not sing
  While yon sun prospers in the blue,
  Shall sing for want, ere leaves are new,
Caught in the frozen palms of spring.

ALFRED, LORD TENNYSON

The Redwing

The winter clenched its fist
And knuckles numb with frost
Struck blind at the blinding snow.
It was hard for domestic creatures,
Cows, humans, and such, to get
Shelter and warmth and food.
And then the redwings came,
Birds of the open field,
The wood, the wild, only
Extremity makes them yield.

I must admit that never
Before that day when thaw
Bled red to white in the west
Had I seen a redwing, but there
Where ivy-berries offered
A last everlasting lost
Hope of life I held
A redwing in my hand,
Still warm, and was it dead?
It had toppled from a tree
Too weak too frail to fill
Its crop before the frost
Again asked for the cost
Of a winter dosshouse rest.
So I saw what it was like.

Never before had I seen
A redwing, now a hundred
Hopped through the shivering town
Unrecognised, unknown
To most who saw them save
Simply as 'birds'. They came
As poets come among us,
Driven in from the wild
Not asking nor expecting
To be recognised for what

They are — if they are not
The usual thrush you can
Identify them dead.

I held it in my hand,
I knew that it was dead,
But still I willed it to live
Not asking nor expecting
Many to understand
Why I must will it so.
But I know what a redwing is,
And I know how I know.

PATRIC DICKINSON

The Throstle

'Summer is coming, summer is coming.
    I know it, I know it, I know it.
Light again, leaf again, life again, love again,'
    Yes, my wild little Poet.

Sing the new year in under the blue.
    Last year you sang it as gladly.
'New, new, new, new'! Is it then *so* new
    That you should carol so madly?

'Love again, song again, nest again, young again.'
    Never a prophet so crazy!
And hardly a daisy as yet, little friend,
    See, there is hardly a daisy.

'Here again, here, here, here, happy year'!
    O warble unchidden, unbidden!
Summer is coming, is coming, my dear,
    And all the winters are hidden.

ALFRED, LORD TENNYSON

[77]

The Darkling Thrush

I leant upon a coppice gate
    When frost was spectre-grey,
And winter's dregs made desolate
    The weakening eye of day.
The tangled bine-stems scored the sky
    Like strings of broken lyres,
And all mankind that haunted nigh
    Had sought their household fires.

The land's sharp features seemed to be
    The century's corpse outleant,
His crypt the cloudy canopy,
    The wind his death-lament.
The ancient pulse of germ and birth
    Was shrunken hard and dry,
And every spirit upon earth
    Seemed fervourless as I.

At once a voice arose among
    The bleak twigs overhead
In a full-hearted evensong
    Of joy illimited;
An agèd thrush, frail, gaunt, and small,
    In blast-beruffled plume,
Had chosen thus to fling his soul
    Upon the growing gloom.

So little cause for carolings
    Of such ecstatic sound
Was written on terrestrial things
    Afar or nigh around,
That I could think there trembled through
    His happy good-night air
Some blessèd hope, whereof he knew
    And I was unaware.

THOMAS HARDY

The Thrush

When Winter's ahead,
What can you read in November
That you read in April
When Winter's dead?

I hear the thrush, and I see
Him alone at the end of the lane
Near the bare poplar's tip,
Singing continuously.

Is it more that you know
Than that, even as in April,
So in November,
Winter is gone that must go?

Or is all your lore
Not to call November November,
And April April,
And Winter Winter — no more?

But I know the months all,
And their sweet names, April,
May and June and October,
As you call and call

I must remember
What died in April
And consider what will be born
Of a fair November;

And April I love for what
It was born of, and November
For what it will die in,
What they are and what they are not.

While you love what is kind,
What you can sing in
And love and forget in
All that's ahead and behind.

EDWARD THOMAS

[79]

Bell-birds

By channels of coolness the echoes are calling,
And down the dim gorges I hear the creek falling:
It lives in the mountain where moss and the sedges
Touch with their beauty the banks and the ledges.
Through breaks of the cedar and sycámore bowers
Struggles the light that is love to the flowers;
And, softer than slumber and sweeter than singing,
The notes of the bell-birds are running and ringing.

The silver-voiced bell-birds, the darlings of daytime!
They sing in September their songs of the May-time;
When shadows wax strong, and the thunder-bolts hurtle,
They hide with their fear in the leaves of the myrtle;
When rain and the sunbeams shine mingled together,
They start up like fairies that follow fair weather;
And straightway the hues of their feathers unfolden
Are the green and the purple, the blue and the golden.

October, the maiden of bright yellow tresses,
Loiters for love in these cool wildernesses;
Loiters, knee-deep, in the grasses, to listen,
Where dripping rocks gleam and the leafy pools glisten:
Then is the time when the water-moons splendid
Break with their gold, and are scattered or blended
Over the creeks, till the woodlands have warning
Of songs of the bell-bird and wings of the Morning.

Welcome as waters unkissed by the summers
Are the voices of bell-birds to thirsty far-comers.
When fiery December sets foot in the forest,
And the need of the wayfarer presses the sorest,
Pent in the ridges for ever and ever
The bell-birds direct him to spring and to river,
With ring and with ripple, like runnels whose torrents
Are toned by the pebbles and leaves in the currents.

Often I sit, looking back to a childhood,
Mixt with the sights and the sounds of the wildwood,
Longing for power and the sweetness to fashion,
Lyrics with beats like the heart-beats of Passion; —
Songs interwoven of lights and of laughters
Borrowed from bell-birds in far forest-rafters;
So I might keep in the city and alleys
The beauty and strength of the deep mountain valleys;
Charming to slumber the pain of my losses
With glimpses of creeks and a vision of mosses.

HENRY KENDALL

A Wren's Nest

Among the dwellings framed by birds
    In field or forest with nice care,
Is none that with the little Wren's
    In snugness may compare.

No door the tenement requires,
    And seldom needs a laboured roof;
Yet is it to the fiercest sun
    Impervious, and storm-proof.

So warm, so beautiful withal,
    In perfect fitness for its aim,
That to the Kind by special grace
    Their instinct surely came.

And when for their abodes they seek
    An opportune recess,
The hermit has no finer eye
    For shadowy quietness.

[81]

These find, mid ivied abbey-walls,
  A canopy in some still nook;
Others are pent-housed by a brae
  That overhangs a brook.

There to the brooding bird her mate
  Warbles by fits his low clear song;
And by the busy streamlet both
  Are sung to all day long.

Or in sequestered lanes they build,
  Where, till the flitting bird's return,
Her eggs within the nest repose,
  Like relics in an urn.

But still, where general choice is good,
  There is a better and a best;
And, among fairest objects, some
  Are fairer than the rest;

This, one of those small builders proved
  In a green covert, where, from out
The forehead of a pollard oak,
  The leafy antlers sprout;

For She who planned the mossy lodge,
  Mistrusting her evasive skill,
Had to a Primrose looked for aid
  Her wishes to fulfil.

High on the trunk's projecting brow,
  And fixed an infant's span above
The budding flowers, peeped forth the nest
  The prettiest of the grove!

The treasure proudly did I show
  To some whose minds without disdain
Can turn to little things; but once
  Looked up for it in vain:

'T is gone — a ruthless spoiler's prey,
  Who heeds not beauty, love, or song,
'T is gone! (so seemed it) and we grieved
  Indignant at the wrong.

Just three days after, passing by
  In clearer light the moss-built cell
I saw, espied its shaded mouth;
  And felt that all was well.

The Primrose for a veil had spread
  The largest of her upright leaves;
And thus, for purposes benign,
  A simple flower deceives.

Concealed from friends who might disturb
  Thy quiet with no ill intent,
Secure from evil eyes and hands
  On barbarous plunder bent,

Rest, Mother-bird! and when thy young
  Take flight, and thou art free to roam,
When withered is the guardian Flower,
  And empty thy late home,

Think how ye prospered, thou and thine,
  Amid the unviolated grove
Housed near the growing Primrose-tuft
  In foresight, or in love.

WILLIAM WORDSWORTH

The Wren

Why is the cuckoo's melody preferred,
   And nightingale's rich songs so madly praised
In poets' rhymes? Is there no other bird
   Of nature's minstrelsy, that oft hath raised
One's heart to ecstasy and mirth as well?
   I judge not how another's taste is caught,
With mine are other birds that bear the bell,
   Whose song hath crowds of happy memories brought:
Such the wood robin, singing in the dell,
   And little wren, that many a time hath sought
Shelter from showers, in huts where I did dwell
   In early spring, the tenant of the plain,
Tenting my sheep; and still they come to tell
   The happy stories of the past again.

JOHN CLARE

The Green Linnet

Beneath these fruit-tree boughs that shed
Their snow-white blossoms on my head,
With brightest sunshine round me spread
   Of spring's unclouded weather,
In this sequestered nook how sweet
To sit upon my orchard-seat!
And birds and flowers once more to greet,
   My last year's friends together.

One have I marked, the happiest guest
In all this covert of the blest:
Hail to Thee, far above the rest
   In joy of voice and pinion!
Thou, Linnet! in thy green array,
Presiding Spirit here to-day,
Dost lead the revels of the May;
   And this is thy dominion.

[84]

While birds, and butterflies, and flowers,
Make all one band of paramours,
Thou, ranging up and down the bowers,
　　Art sole in thy employment:
A Life, a Presence like the Air,
Scattering thy gladness without care,
Too blest with any one to pair;
　　Thyself thy own enjoyment.

Amid yon tuft of hazel trees
That twinkle to the gusty breeze,
Behold him perched in ecstasies,
　　Yet seeming still to hover;
There! where the flutter of his wings
Upon his back and body flings
Shadows and sunny glimmerings,
　　That cover him all over.

My dazzled sight he oft deceives,
A Brother of the dancing leaves;
Then flits, and from the cottage-eaves
　　Pours forth his song in gushes;
As if by that exulting strain
He mocked and treated with disdain
The voiceless Form he chose to feign,
　　While fluttering in the bushes.

WILLIAM WORDSWORTH

The Linnet in November

Late singer of a sunless day,
　I know not if with pain
Or pleasure more, I hear thy lay
　Renew its vernal strain.

As gleams of youth, when youth is o'er,
   And bare the summer bowers,
Thy song brings back the years of yore,
   And unreturning hours.

So was it once! So yet again
   It never more will be!
Yet sing; and lend us in thy strain
   A moment's youth with thee.

F. T. PALGRAVE

'I heard a linnet courting'

I heard a linnet courting
   His lady in the spring:
His mates were idly sporting,
   Nor stayed to hear him sing
     His song of love. —
I fear my speech distorting
     His tender love.

The phrases of his pleading
   Were full of young delight;
And she that gave him heeding
   Interpreted aright
     His gay, sweet notes, —
So sadly marred in the reading, —
     His tender notes.

And when he ceased, the hearer
   Awaited the refrain,
Till swiftly perching nearer
   He sang his song again,
     His pretty song: —
Would that my verse spake clearer
     His tender song!

BIRDS

Ye happy, airy creatures!
    That in the merry spring
Think not of what misfeatures
    Or cares the year may bring;
        But unto love
Resign your simple natures
        To tender love.

ROBERT BRIDGES

The Jackdaw

There is a bird who, by his coat,
And by the hoarseness of his note,
    Might be supposed a crow;
A great frequenter of the church,
Where, bishop-like, he finds a perch,
    And dormitory too.

Above the steeple shines a plate,
That turns and turns, to indicate
    From what point blows the weather.
Look up — your brains begin to swim,
'Tis in the clouds — that pleases him,
    He chooses it the rather.

Fond of the speculative height,
Thither he wings his airy flight,
    And thence securely sees
The bustle and the raree-show
That occupy mankind below,
    Secure and at his ease.

You think, no doubt, he sits and muses
On future broken bones and bruises,
    If he should chance to fall.
No; not a single thought like that
Employs his philosophic pate,
    Or troubles it at all.

[87]

He sees that this great roundabout —
The world, with all its motley rout,
   Church, army, physic, law,
Its customs, and its bus'nesses —
Is no concern at all of his,
   And says — what says he? — Caw.

Thrice happy bird! I too have seen
Much of the vanities of men;
   And, sick of having seen 'em,
Would cheerfully these limbs resign
For such a pair of wings as thine,
   And such a head between 'em.

WILLIAM COWPER

The Bird

Hither thou com'st; the busy wind all night
Blew through thy lodging, where thy own warm wing
Thy pillow was. Many a sullen storm,
For which course man seems much the fitter born,
   Rain'd on thy bed
   And harmless head;

And now as fresh and cheerful as the light
Thy little heart in early hymns doth sing
Unto that *Providence*, whose unseen arm
Curb'd them, and clothed thee well and warm.
   All things that be, praise Him; and had
   Their lesson taught them when first made.

So hills and valleys into singing break,
And though poor stones have neither speech nor tongue,
While active winds and streams both run and speak,
Yet stones are deep in admiration.
Thus Praise and Prayer here beneath the sun
Make lesser mornings, when the great are done.

[88]

For each enclosed spirit is a star
    Inlightning his own little sphere,
Whose light, though fetched and borrowed from afar,
    Both mornings makes and evenings there.

HENRY VAUGHAN

The Flight of Birds

The crow goes flopping on from wood to wood,
The wild duck wherries to the distant flood,
The starnels hurry o'er in merry crowds,
And overhead whew by like hasty clouds;
The wild duck from the meadow-water plies
And dashes up the water as he flies;
The pigeon suthers by on rapid wing,
The lark mounts upward at the call of spring.
In easy flights above the hurricane
With doubled neck high sails the noisy crane.
Whizz goes the pewit o'er the ploughman's team,
With many a whew and whirl and sudden scream;
And lightly fluttering to the tree just by,
In chattering journeys whirls the noisy pie;
From bush to bush slow swees the screaming jay,
With one harsh note of pleasure all the day.

JOHN CLARE

Proud Songsters

The thrushes sing as the sun is going,
    And the finches whistle in ones and pairs,
And as it gets dark loud nightingales
    In bushes
Pipe, as they can when April wears,
    As if all Time were theirs.

BIRDS

These are brand-new birds of twelve-months' growing,
Which a year ago, or less than twain,
No finches were, nor nightingales,
        Nor thrushes,
But only particles of grain,
    And earth, and air, and rain.

THOMAS HARDY

Birds' Nests

The summer nests uncovered by autumn wind,
Some torn, others dislodged, all dark,
Everyone sees them: low or high in tree,
Or hedge, or single bush, they hang like a mark.

Since there's no need of eyes to see them with
I cannot help a little shame
That I missed most, even at eye's level, till
The leaves blew off and made the seeing no game.

'Tis a light pang. I like to see the nests
Still in their places, now first known,
At home and by far roads. Boys knew them not,
Whatever jays and squirrels may have done.

And most I like the winter nests deep hid
That leaves and berries fell into:
Once a dormouse dined there on hazel-nuts,
And grass and goose-grass seeds found soil and grew.

EDWARD THOMAS

The Feather

I stoop to gather a seabird's feather
Fallen on the beach,
Torn from a beautiful drifting wing;
What can I learn or teach,
Running my finger through the comb
And along the horny quill?
The body it was torn from
Gave out a cry so shrill,
Sailors looked from their white road
To see what help was there.
It dragged the winds to a drop of blood
Falling through drowned air,
Dropping from the sea-hawk's beak,
From frenzied talons sharp;
Now if the words they lost I speak
It must be to that harp
Under the strange, light-headed sea
That bears a straw of the nest.
Unless I make that melody,
How can the dead have rest?

Sheer from wide air to the wilderness
The victim fell, and lay;
The starlike bone is fathomless,
Lost among wind and spray.
This lonely, isolated thing
Trembles amid their sound.
I set my finger on the string
That spins the ages round.
But let it sleep, let it sleep
Where shell and stone are cast;
Its ecstasy the Furies keep,
For nothing here is past.
The perfect into night must fly;
On this the winds agree.
How could a blind rock satisfy
The hungers of the sea?

VERNON WATKINS

[91]

Section 2

PLANTS AND TREES

To Blossoms

Fair pledges of a fruitful tree,
  Why do ye fall so fast?
  Your date is not so past
But you may stay yet here awhile
  To blush and gently smile,
    And go at last.

What! were ye born to be
  An hour or half's delight,
  And so to bid good night?
'Twas pity Nature brought you forth
  Merely to show your worth
    And lose you quite.

But you are lovely leaves, where we
  May read how soon things have
  Their end, though ne'er so brave:
And after they have shown their pride
  Like you awhile, they glide
    Into the grave.

ROBERT HERRICK

To Violets

Welcome, maids of honour!
  You do bring
  In the spring,
And await upon her.

She has virgins many,
  Fresh and fair;
  Yet you are
More sweet than any.

[95]

You're the maiden posies,
    And so graced
    To be placed
'Fore damask roses.

Yet, though thus respected,
    By-and-by
    Ye do lie,
Poor girls, neglected.

ROBERT HERRICK

To Daffodils

Fair daffodils, we weep to see
    You haste away so soon;
As yet the early-rising sun
    Has not attain'd his noon.
        Stay, stay
      Until the hasting day
        Has run
      But to the evensong;
And, having pray'd together, we
    Will go with you along.

We have short time to stay, as you,
    We have as short a spring;
As quick a growth to meet decay,
    As you, or anything.
        We die
      As your hours do, and dry
        Away
      Like to the summer's rain;
Or as the pearls of morning's dew,
    Ne'er to be found again.

ROBERT HERRICK

[96]

'I wandered lonely as a cloud'

I wandered lonely as a cloud
That floats on high o'er vales and hills,
When all at once I saw a crowd,
A host, of golden daffodils;
Beside the lake, beneath the trees,
Fluttering and dancing in the breeze.

Continuous as the stars that shine
And twinkle on the milky way,
They stretched in never-ending line
Along the margin of a bay:
Ten thousand saw I at a glance,
Tossing their heads in sprightly dance.

The waves beside them danced; but they
Out-did the sparkling waves in glee:
A poet could not but be gay,
In such a jocund company:
I gazed — and gazed — but little thought
What wealth the show to me had brought:

For oft, when on my couch I lie
In vacant or in pensive mood,
They flash upon that inward eye
Which is the bliss of solitude;
And then my heart with pleasure fills,
And dances with the daffodils.

WILLIAM WORDSWORTH

To a Snow-drop

Lone Flower, hemmed in with snows and white as they
But hardier far, once more I see thee bend
Thy forehead, as if fearful to offend,
Like an unbidden guest. Though, day by day
Storms, sallying from the mountain-tops, waylay
The rising sun, and on the plains descend;
Yet art thou welcome, welcome as a friend
Whose zeal outruns his promise! Blue-eyed May
Shall soon behold this border thickly set
With bright jonquils, their odours lavishing
On the soft west-wind and his frolic peers;
Nor will I then thy modest grace forget,
Chaste Snow-drop, venturous harbinger of Spring,
And pensive monitor of fleeting years!

WILLIAM WORDSWORTH

To the Small Celandine

Pansies, lilies, kingcups, daisies,
Let them live upon their praises;
Long as there's a sun that sets,
Primroses will have their glory;
Long as there are violets,
They will have a place in story:
There's a flower that shall be mine,
'Tis the little Celandine.

Eyes of some men travel far
For the finding of a star;
Up and down the heavens they go,
Men that keep a mighty rout!
I'm as great as they, I trow,
Since the day I found thee out,
Little Flower! — I'll make a stir,
Like a sage astronomer.

[98]

PLANTS AND TREES

Modest, yet withal an Elf
Bold, and lavish of thyself;
Since we needs must first have met
I have seen thee, high and low,
Thirty years or more, and yet
'Twas a face I did not know;
Thou hast now, go where I may,
Fifty greetings in a day.

Ere a leaf is on a bush,
In the time before the thrush
Has a thought about her nest,
Thou wilt come with half a call,
Spreading out thy glossy breast
Like a careless Prodigal;
Telling tales about the sun,
When we've little warmth, or none.

Poets, vain men in their mood!
Travel with the multitude:
Never heed them; I aver
That they all are wanton wooers;
But the thrifty cottager,
Who stirs little out of doors,
Joy to spy thee near her home;
Spring is coming, Thou art come!

Comfort have thou of thy merit,
Kindly, unassuming Spirit!
Careless of thy neighbourhood,
Thou dost show thy pleasant face
On the moor, and in the wood,
In the lane; — there's not a place,
Howsoever mean it be,
But 'tis good enough for thee.

Ill befall the yellow flowers,
Children of the flaring hours!
Buttercups, that will be seen,
Whether we will see or no;

[99]

Others, too, of lofty mien;
They have done as worldlings do,
Taken praise that should be thine,
Little, humble Celandine!

Prophet of delight and mirth,
Ill-requited upon earth;
Herald of a mighty band,
Of a joyous train ensuing,
Serving at my heart's command,
Tasks that are no tasks renewing,
I will sing, as doth behove,
Hymns in praise of what I love!

WILLIAM WORDSWORTH

To the Daisy

With little here to do or see
Of things that in the great world be,
Daisy! again I talk to thee,
      For thou art worthy,
Thou unassuming Common-place
Of Nature, with that homely face,
And yet with something of a grace,
      Which Love makes for thee!

Oft on the dappled turf at ease
I sit, and play with similies,
Loose types of things through all degrees,
      Thoughts of thy raising:
And many a fond and idle name
I give to thee, for praise or blame,
As is the humour of the game,
      While I am gazing.

[100]

A nun demure of lowly port;
Or sprightly maiden, of Love's court,
In thy simplicity the sport
 Of all temptations;
A queen in crown of rubies drest;
A starveling in a scanty vest;
Are all, as seems to suit thee best,
  Thy appellations.

A little cyclops, with one eye
Staring to threaten and defy,
That thought comes next — and instantly
 The freak is over,
The shape will vanish — and behold
A silver shield with boss of gold,
That spreads itself, some faery bold
  In fight to cover!

I see thee glittering from afar —
And then thou art a pretty star;
Not quite so fair as many are
 In heaven above thee!
Yet like a star, with glittering crest,
Self-poised in air thou seem'st to rest; —
May peace come never to his nest,
  Who shall reprove thee!

Bright *Flower!* for by that name at last,
When all my reveries are past,
I call thee, and to that cleave fast,
 Sweet silent creature!
That breath'st with me in sun and air,
Do thou, as thou art wont, repair
My heart with gladness, and a share
  Of thy meek nature!

WILLIAM WORDSWORTH

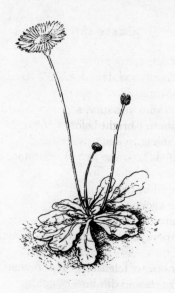

To a Daisy

Slight as thou art, thou art enough to hide
    Like all created things, secrets from me,
And stand a barrier to eternity.
And I, how can I praise thee well and wide

From where I dwell — upon the hither side?
    Thou little veil for so great mystery,
    When shall I penetrate all things and thee,
And then look back? For this I must abide,

Till thou shalt grow and fold and be unfurled
Literally between me and the world.
    Then I shall drink from in beneath a spring,

And from a poet's side shall read his book.
    O daisy mine, what will it be to look
    From God's side even of such a simple thing?

ALICE MEYNELL

The Daisy

Having so rich a treasury, so fine a hoard
Of beauty water-bright before my eyes,
I plucked the daisy only, simple and white
In its fringed frock and brooch of innocent gold.

So is all equilibrium restored:
I leave the noontide wealth of richer bloom
To the destroyer, the impatient ravisher,
The intemperate bee, the immoderate bird.

Of all this beauty felt and seen and heard
I can be frugal and devout and plain,
Deprived so long of light and air and grass,
The shyest flower is sweetest to uncover.

How poor I was: and yet no richer lover
Discovered joy so deep in earth and water;
And in the air that fades from blue to pearl,
And in a flower white-frocked like my small daughter.

MARYA ZATURENSKA

The Wild Honey Suckle

Fair flower, that dost so comely grow,
Hid in this silent, dull retreat,
Untouched thy honied blossoms blow,
Unseen thy little branches greet:
    No roving foot shall crush thee here,
    No busy hand provoke a tear.

By Nature's self in white arrayed,
She bade thee shun the vulgar eye,
And planted here the guardian shade,
And sent soft waters murmuring by;
  Thus quietly thy summer goes,
  Thy days declining to repose.

Smit with those charms, that must decay,
I grieve to see your future doom;
They died — nor were those flowers more gay,
The flowers that did in Eden bloom;
  Unpitying frosts, and Autumn's power
  Shall leave no vestige of this flower.

From morning suns and evening dews
At first thy little being came:
If nothing once, you nothing lose,
For when you die you are the same;
  The space between, is but an hour,
  The frail duration of a flower.

PHILIP FRENEAU

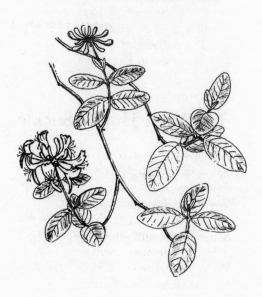

The Lent Lily

'Tis spring; come out to ramble
  The hilly brakes around,
For under thorn and bramble
  About the hollow ground
  The primroses are found.

And there's the windflower chilly
  With all the winds at play,
And there's the Lenten lily
  That has not long to stay
  And dies on Easter day.

And since till girls go maying
  You find the primrose still,
And find the windflower playing
  With every wind at will,
  But not the daffodil,

Bring baskets now, and sally
  Upon the spring's array,
And bear from hill and valley
  The daffodil away
  That dies on Easter day.

A. E. HOUSMAN

Poppies

We are slumberous poppies,
  Lords of Lethe downs,
Some awake, and some asleep,
  Sleeping in our crowns.
What perchance our dreams may know,
Let our serious beauty show.

[105]

Central depth of purple
    Leaves more bright than rose,
Who shall tell what brightest thought
    Out of darkest grows?
Who, through what funereal pain
Souls to love and peace attain?

Visions aye are on us,
    Unto eyes of power,
Pluto's always setting sun,
    And Proserpine's bower:
There, like bees, the pale souls come
For our drink with drowsy hum.

Taste, ye mortals, also;
    Milky-hearted, we;
Taste, but with a reverent care;
    Active-patient be.
Too much gladness brings to gloom
Those who on the gods presume.

LEIGH HUNT

The Sick Rose

O Rose! thou art sick!
The invisible worm,
That flies in the night,
In the howling storm,

Has found out thy bed
Of crimson joy;
And his dark secret love
Does thy life destroy.

WILLIAM BLAKE

A Rose-bud by my Early Walk

A rose-bud by my early walk,
Adown a corn-enclosèd bawk,
Sae gently bent its thorny stalk,
   All on a dewy morning.

Ere twice the shades o' dawn are fled,
In a' its crimson glory spread,
And drooping rich the dewy head,
   It scents the early morning.

Within the bush, her covert nest
A little linnet fondly prest,
The dew sat chilly on her breast
   Sae early in the morning.

She soon shall see her tender brood,
The pride, the pleasure o' the wood,
Amang the fresh green leaves bedew'd.
   Awake the early morning.

So thou, dear bird, young Jeany fair,
On trembling string or vocal air,
Shalt sweetly pay the tender care
   That tents thy early morning.

So thou, sweet rose-bud, young and gay,
Shalt beauteous blaze upon the day,
And bless the parent's evening ray
   That watch'd thy early morning.

ROBERT BURNS

The Wild Rose and the Snowdrop

The Snowdrop is the prophet of the flowers;
It lives and dies upon its bed of snows;
And like a thought of spring it comes and goes,
Hanging its head beside our leafless bowers.
The sun's betrothing kiss it never knows,
Nor all the glowing joy of golden showers;
But ever in a placid, pure repose,
More like a spirit with its look serene,
Droops its pale cheek veined thro' with infant green.

Queen of her sisters is the sweet Wild Rose,
Sprung from the earnest sun and ripe young June;
The year's own darling and the Summer's Queen!
Lustrous as the new-throned crescent moon.
Much of that early prophet look she shows,
Mixed with her fair espoused blush which glows,
As if the ethereal fairy blood were seen;
Like a soft evening over sunset snows,
Half twilight violet shade, half crimson sheen.

Twin-born are both in beauteousness, most fair
In all that glads the eye and charms the air;
In all that wakes emotions in the mind
And sows sweet sympathies for human kind.
Twin-born, albeit their seasons are apart,
They bloom together in the thoughtful heart;
Fair symbols of the marvels of our state,
Mute speakers of the oracles of fate!
For each, fulfilling nature's law, fulfils
Itself and its own aspirations pure;
Living and dying; letting faith ensure
New life when deathless Spring shall touch the hills.
Each perfect in its place; and each content
With that perfection which its being meant:
Divided not by months that intervene,
But linked by all the flowers that bud between.

Forever smiling thro' its season brief,
The one in glory and the one in grief:
Forever painting to our museful sight,
How lowlihead and loveliness unite.

Born from the first blind yearning of the earth
To be a mother and give happy birth,
Ere yet the northern sun such rapture brings,
Lo, from her virgin breast the Snowdrop springs;
And ere the snows have melted from the grass,
And not a strip of greensward doth appear,
Save the faint prophecy its cheeks declare,
Alone, unkissed, unloved, behold it pass!
While in the ripe enthronement of the year,
Whispering the breeze, and wedding the rich air
With her so sweet, delicious bridal breath, —
Odorous and exquisite beyond compare,
And starr'd with dews upon her forehead clear,
Fresh-hearted as a Maiden Queen should be
Who takes the land's devotion as her fee, —
The Wild Rose blooms, all summer for her dower,
Nature's most beautiful and perfect flower.

GEORGE MEREDITH

The Ivy Green

Oh, a dainty plant is the Ivy green,
That creepeth o'er ruins old!
Of right choice food are his meals, I ween,
In his cell so lone and cold.
The wall must be crumbled, the stone decayed,
To pleasure his dainty whim:
And the mouldering dust that years have made
Is a merry meal for him.
Creeping where no life is seen,
A rare old plant is the Ivy green.

[109]

Fast he stealeth on, though he wears no wings,
And a staunch old heart has he.
How closely he twineth, how tight he clings,
To his friend the hugh Oak Tree!
And slily he traileth along the ground,
And his leaves he gently waves,
As he joyously hugs and crawleth round
The rich mould of dead men's graves.
    Creeping where grim death hath been,
    A rare old plant is the Ivy green.

Whole ages have fled and their works decayed,
And nations have scattered been;
But the stout old Ivy shall never fade,
From its hale and hearty green.
The brave old plant, in its lonely days,
Shall fatten upon the past:
For the stateliest building man can raise
Is the Ivy's food at last.
    Creeping on, where time has been,
    A rare old plant is the Ivy green.

CHARLES DICKENS

Thistledown

This might have been a place for sleep
But, as from that small hollow there
Hosts of bright thistledown begin
Their dazzling journey through the air,
An idle man can only stare.

They grip their withered edge of stalk
In brief excitement for the wind;
They hold a breathless final talk,
And when their filmy cables part
One almost hears a little cry.

[110]

Some cling together while they wait
And droop and gaze and hesitate,
But others leap along the sky,
Or circle round and calmly choose
The gust they know they ought to use.

While some in loving pairs will glide,
Or watch the others as they pass,
Or rest on flowers in the grass,
Or circle through the shining day
Like silvery butterflies at play.

Some catch themselves to every mound,
Then lingeringly and slowly move
As if they knew the precious ground
Were opening for their fertile love:
They almost try to dig, they need
So much to plant their thistle-seed.

HAROLD MONRO

To the Dandelion

Dear common flower, that grow'st beside the way,
Fringing the dusty road with harmless gold,
First pledge of blithesome May,
Which children pluck, and, full of pride uphold,
High-hearted buccaneers, o'erjoyed that they
An Eldorado in the grass have found,
Which not the rich earth's ample round
May match in wealth, thou art more dear to me
Than all the prouder summer-blooms may be.

Gold such as thine ne'er drew the Spanish prow
Through the primeval hush of Indian seas,
Nor wrinkled the lean brow
Of age, to rob the lover's heart of ease;

'Tis the Spring's largess, which she scatters now
To rich and poor alike, with lavish hand,
    Though most hearts never understand
  To take it at God's value, but pass by
The offered wealth with unrewarded eye.

Thou art my tropics and mine Italy;
To look at thee unlocks a warmer clime;
    The eyes thou givest me
Are in the heart, and heed not space or time:
  Not in mid June the golden-cuirassed bee
Feels a more summer-like warm ravishment
    In the white lily's breezy tent,
  His fragrant Sybaris, than I, when first
From the dark green thy yellow circles burst.

Then think I of deep shadows on the grass,
Of meadows where in sun the cattle graze,
    Where, as the breezes pass,
The gleaming rushes lean a thousand ways,
  Of leaves that slumber in a cloudy mass,
Or whiten in the wind, of waters blue
    That from the distance sparkle through
  Some woodland gap, and of a sky above,
Where one white cloud like a stray lamb doth move.

My childhood's earliest thoughts are linked with thee;
The sight of thee calls back the robin's song,
    Who, from the dark old tree
Beside the door, sang clearly all day long;
  And I, secure in childish piety,
Listened as if I heard an angel sing
    With news from heaven, which he could bring
  Fresh every day to my untainted ears
When birds and flowers and I were happy peers.

How like a prodigal doth nature seem,
When thou, for all thy gold, so common art!
   Thou teachest me to deem
More sacredly of every human heart,
  Since each reflects in joy its scanty gleam
Of heaven, and could some wondrous secret show,
    Did we but pay the love we owe,
  And with a child's undoubting wisdom look
On all these living pages of God's book.

JAMES RUSSELL LOWELL

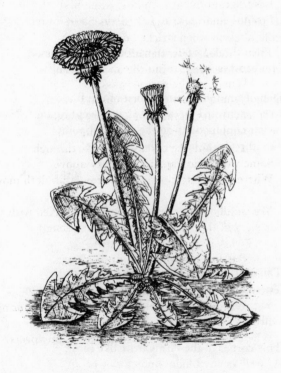

The Air Plant

(Grand Cayman, W.I.)

This tuft that thrives on saline nothingness,
Inverted octopus with heavenward arms
Thrust parching from a palm-bole hard by the cove —
A bird almost — of almost bird alarms,

Is pulmonary to the wind that jars
Its tentacles, horrific in their lurch.
The lizard's throat, held bloated for a fly,
Balloons but warily from this throbbing perch.

The needles and hacksaws of cactus bleed
A milk of earth when stricken off the stalk;
But this — defenseless, thornless, sheds no blood,
Scarce shadow even — but the air's thin talk.

Angelic Dynamo! Ventriloquist of the Blue!
While beachward creeps the shark-swept Spanish Main.
By what conjunctions do the winds appoint
Its apotheosis, at last — the hurricane!

HART CRANE

Tall Nettles

Tall nettles cover up, as they have done
These many springs, the rusty harrow, the plough
Long worn out, and the roller made of stone:
Only the elm butt tops the nettles now.

This corner of the farmyard I like most:
As well as any bloom upon a flower
I like the dust on the nettles, never lost
Except to prove the sweetness of a shower.

EDWARD THOMAS

A Contemplation upon Flowers

Brave flowers, that I could gallant it like you
And be as little vaine,
You come abroad, and make a harmelesse shew,
And to your beds of Earthe againe;
You are not proud, you know your birth
For your Embroider'd garments are from Earth:

You doe obey your months, and times, but I
Would have it ever spring,
My fate would know no winter, never die
Nor thinke of such a thing;
Oh that I could my bed of Earth but view
And Smile, and looke as Chearefully as you:

Oh teach me to see Death, and not to fear
But rather to take truce;
How often have I seene you at a Bier,
And there look fresh and spruce;
You fragrant flowers, then teach me that my breath
Like yours may sweeten, and perfume my Death.

HENRY KING

Flowers

Yes; there is heaven about you: in your breath
    And hues it dwells. The stars of heaven ye shine;
Bright strangers in a land of sin and death,
    That talk of God, and point to realms divine. . . .

Ye speak of frail humanity: ye tell
    How man, like you, shall flourish and shall fall: —
But ah! ye speak of Heavenly Love as well,
    And say, the God of flowers is God of all. . . .

[115]

Sweet flowers, sweet flowers! the rich exuberance
   Of Nature's heart in her propitious hours:
When glad emotions in her bosom dance
   She vents her happiness in laughing flowers. . . .

Childhood and you are playmates; matching well
   Your sunny cheeks, and mingling fragrant breath: —
Ye help young Love his faltering tale to tell;
   Ye scatter sweetness o'er the bed of Death.

HENRY FRANCIS LYTE

Field Flowers

Ye field flowers! the gardens eclipse you, 'tis true,
Yet, wildings of nature, I doat upon you;
   For ye waft me to summers of old,
When the earth teemed around me with fairy delight,
And when daisies and buttercups gladdened my sight,
   Like treasures of silver and gold.

I love you for lulling me back into dreams
Of the blue Highland mountains and echoing streams,
   And of broken glades breathing their balm,
While the deer was seen glancing in sunshine remote,
And the deep mellow crush of the wood-pigeon's note
   Made music that sweetened the calm.

Not a pastoral song has a pleasanter tune
Than ye speak to my heart, little wildings of June:
   Of old ruinous castles ye tell,
Where I thought it delightful your beauties to find,
When the magic of Nature first breathed on my mind,
   And your blossoms were part of her spell.

Even now what affections the violet awakes;
What loved little islands twice seen in their lakes,
  Can the wild water-lily restore;
What landscapes I read in the primrose's looks,
And what pictures of pebbled and minnowy brooks
  In the vetches that tangled their shore.

Earth's cultureless buds, to my heart ye were dear,
Ere the fever of passion or ague of fear
  Had scathed my existence's bloom;
Once I welcome you more, in life's passionless stage,
With the visions of youth to revisit my age,
  And I wish you to grow on my tomb.

THOMAS CAMPBELL

Moss

'Patents' will burn it out; it would lie there
Turning white. It shelters on the soil; quilts it.
So persons lie over it; but look closely:
The thick, short green threads quiver like an animal
As a fungoid quivers between that and vegetable:
A mushroom's flesh with the texture and consistency of a kidney.
Moss is soft as a pouch.

There are too many shoots though, boxed compacted,
Yet nestling together,
Softly luminous.
They squirm minutely. The less compact kind
Has struggling white flowers; closed,
Like a minute bell's clapper;
So minute that opened then, its stretch seems wide.
The first grows in damper places.

[117]

With what does it propagate?
Quiet, of course, it adheres to
The cracks of waste-pipes, velvets,
Velours them; an enriching
Unnatural ruff swathing the urban 'manifestation':
The urban nature is basemented, semi-dark;
It musts, it is alone.

Here moss cools; it has no children;
It amplifies itself.
Could that over-knit fiction of stubbed threads reproduce
Defined creatures?
It hovers tentatively between one life and another,
Being the closed-road of plants,
Its mule; spreads only its kind —
A soft stone. It is not mad.
Reared on the creeping dankness of the earth
It overspreads, smears, begrudges something
Though it is passive; spreads wildly.
It is immune to nothing;
You cannot speak of misery to it.

JON SILKIN

The Tree

Fair *Tree!* for thy delightful Shade
'Tis just that some Return be made:
Sure, some Return is due from me
To thy cool Shadows, and to thee.
When thou to *Birds* do'st Shelter give,
Thou Musick do'st from them receive;
If *Travellers* beneath thee stay,
'Till Storms have worn themselves away,
That Time in praising thee they spend,
And thy protecting Pow'r commend:
The *Shepherd* here, from Scorching freed,
Tunes to thy dancing Leaves his Reed;

[118]

Whilst his lov'd Nymph, in Thanks, bestows
Her flow'ry Chaplets on thy Boughs.
Shall I then only Silent be,
And no Return be made by me?
No; let this Wish upon thee wait,
And still to flourish be thy Fate,
To future Ages may'st thou stand
Untouch'd by the rash Workman's hand;
'Till that large Stock of Sap is spent,
Which gives thy Summer's Ornament;
'Till the fierce Winds, that vainly strive
To shock thy Greatness whilst alive,
Shall on thy lifeless Hour attend,
Prevent the Axe, and grace thy End;
Their scatter'd Strength together call,
And to the Clouds proclaim thy Fall;
Who then their Ev'ning-Dews may spare,
When thou no longer art their Care;
But shalt, like ancient Heroes, burn,
And some bright Hearth be made thy Urn.

ANNE, COUNTESS OF WINCHILSEA

Willow

The feathers of the willow
Are half of them grown yellow
    Above the swelling stream;
And ragged are the bushes,
And rusty now the rushes,
    And wild the clouded gleam.

The thistle now is older,
His stalk begins to moulder,
    His head is white as snow;
The branches all are barer,
The linnet's song is rarer,
    The robin pipeth now.

RICHARD WATSON DIXON

[119]

from

A Forest Hymn

The groves were God's first temples. Ere man learned
To hew the shaft, and lay the architrave,
And spread the roof above them — ere he framed
The lofty vault, to gather and roll back
The sound of anthems; in the darkling wood,
Amid the cool and silence, he knelt down,
And offered to the Mightiest solemn thanks
And supplication. For his simple heart
Might not resist the sacred influences
Which, from the stilly twilight of the place,
And from the gray old trunks that high in heaven
Mingled their mossy boughs, and from the sound
Of the invisible breath that swayed at once
All their green tops, stole over him, and bowed
His spirit with the thought of boundless power
And inaccessible majesty. Ah why
Should we, in the world's riper years, neglect
God's ancient sanctuaries, and adore
Only among the crowd, and under roofs
That our frail hands have raised? Let me, at least,
Here, in the shadow of this aged wood,
Offer one hymn — thrice happy, if it find
Acceptance in His ear.

Father, thy hand
Hath reared these venerable columns, thou
Didst weave this verdant roof. Thou didst look down
Upon the naked earth, and, forthwith, rose
All these fair ranks of trees. They, in thy sun,
Budded, and shook their green leaves in thy breeze,
And shot toward heaven. The century-living crow
Whose birth was in their tops, grew old and died
Among their branches, till, at last, they stood,
As now they stand, massy, and tall, and dark,

Fit shrine for humble worshipper to hold
Communion with his Maker. These dim vaults,
These winding aisles, of human pomp or pride
Report not. No fantastic carvings show
The boast of our vain race to change the form
Of thy fair works. But thou art here — thou fill'st
The solitude. Thou art in the soft winds
That run along the summit of these trees
In music; thou art in the cooler breath
That from the inmost darkness of the place
Comes, scarcely felt; the barky trunks, the ground,
The fresh moist ground, are all instinct with thee.
Here is continual worship; — Nature, here,
In the tranquillity that thou dost love,
Enjoys thy presence. Noiselessly, around,
From perch to perch, the solitary bird
Passes; and yon clear spring, that, midst its herbs,
Wells softly forth and wandering steeps the roots
Of half the mighty forest, tells no tale
Of all the good it does. Thou hast not left
Thyself without a witness, in the shades,
Of thy perfections. Grandeur, strength, and grace
Are here to speak of thee. This mighty oak —
By whose immovable stem I stand and seem
Almost annihilated — not a prince,
In all that proud old world beyond the deep,
E'er wore his crown as loftily as he
Wears the green coronal of leaves with which
Thy hand has graced him. Nestled at his root
Is beauty, such as blooms not in the glare
Of the broad sun. That delicate forest flower,
With scented breath and look so like a smile,
Seems, as it issues from the shapeless mould,
An emanation of the indwelling Life,
A visible token of the upholding Love,
That are the soul of this great universe.

WILLIAM CULLEN BRYANT

[121]

Inscription for
the Entrance to a Wood

Stranger, if thou hast learned a truth which needs
No school of long experience, that the world
Is full of guilt and misery, and hast seen
Enough of all its sorrows, crimes, and cares,
To tire thee of it, enter this wild wood
And view the haunts of Nature. The calm shade
Shall bring a kindred calm, and the sweet breeze
That makes the green leaves dance, shall waft a balm
To thy sick heart. Thou wilt find nothing here
Of all that pained thee in the haunts of men,
And made thee loathe thy life. The primal curse
Fell, it is true, upon the unsinning earth,
But not in vengeance. God hath yoked to guilt
Her pale tormentor, misery. Hence, these shades
Are still the abodes of gladness; the thick roof
Of green and stirring branches is alive
And musical with birds, that sing and sport
In wantonness of spirit; while below
The squirrel, with raised paws and form erect,
Chirps merrily. Throngs of insects in the shade
Try their thin wings and dance in the warm beam
That waked them into life. Even the green trees
Partake the deep contentment; as they bend
To the soft winds, the sun from the blue sky
Looks in and sheds a blessing on the scene.
Scarce less the cleft-born wild-flower seems to enjoy
Existence than the wingèd plunderer
That sucks its sweets. The mossy rocks themselves,
And the old and ponderous trunks of prostrate trees
That lead from knoll to knoll a causey rude
Or bridge the sunken brook, and their dark roots,
With all their earth upon them, twisting high,
Breathe fixed tranquillity. The rivulet
Sends forth glad sounds, and tripping o'er its bed
Of pebbly sands, or leaping down the rocks,

Seems, with continuous laughter, to rejoice
In its own being. Softly tread the marge,
Lest from her midway perch thou scare the wren
That dips her bill in water. The cool wind,
That stirs the stream in play, shall come to thee,
Like one that loves thee nor will let thee pass
Ungreeted, and shall give its light embrace.

WILLIAM CULLEN BRYANT

The Woodlands

O spread agen your leaves an' flow'rs,
   Luonesome woodlands! zunny woodlands!
Here undernēath the dewy show'rs
   O warm-âir'd spring-time, zunny woodlands.
As when, in drong ar oben groun',
Wi' happy buoyish heart I voun'
The twitt'ren birds a' builden roun'
   Your high-bough'd hedges, zunny woodlands.

Ya gie'd me life, ya gie'd me jày,
   Luonesome woodlands, zunny woodlands;
Ya gie'd me health as in my plây
   I rambled droo ye, zunny woodlands.
Ya gie'd me freedom var to rove
In âiry meäd, ar shiady grove;
Ya gie'd me smilen Fanny's love,
   The best ov al ō't, zunny woodlands.

My vust shrill skylark whiver'd high,
   Luonesome woodlands, zunny woodlands.
To zing below your deep-blue sky
   An' white spring-clouds, O zunny woodlands,
An' boughs o' trees that oonce stood here,
Wer glossy green the happy year
That gie'd me oon I lov'd so dear
   An' now ha lost, O zunny woodlands.

[123]

O let me rove agen unspied,
   Luonesome woodlands, zunny woodlands,
Along your green-bough'd hedges' zide,
   As then I rambled, zunny woodlands.
An' wher the missèn trees oonce stood,
Ar tongues oonce rung among the wood,
My memory shall miake em good,
   Though you've a-lost em, zunny woodlands.

WILLIAM BARNES

To a Tree in London

(*Clement's Inn*)

Here you stay
Night and day,
Never, never going away!

Do you ache
When we take
Holiday for our health's sake?

Wish for feet
When the heat
Scalds you in the brick-built street,

That you might
Climb the height
Where your ancestry saw light,

Find a brook
In some nook
There to purge your swarthy look?

No. You read
Trees to need
Smoke like earth whereon to feed. . . .

Have no sense
That far hence
Air is sweet in a blue immense,

Thus, black, blind,
You have opined
Nothing of your brightest kind;

Never seen
Miles of green,
Smelt the landscape's sweet serene.

THOMAS HARDY

[125]

Dirge in Woods

A wind sways the pines,
    And below
Not a breath of wild air;
Still as the mosses that glow
On the flooring and over the lines
Of the roots here and there.

The pine-tree drops its dead;
They are quiet, as under the sea.
Overhead, overhead
Rushes life in a race,
As the clouds the clouds chase;
        And we go,
And we drop like the fruits of the tree,
        Even we,
        Even so.

GEORGE MEREDITH

'Loveliest of trees, the cherry now'

Loveliest of trees, the cherry now
Is hung with bloom along the bough,
And stands about the woodland ride
Wearing white for Eastertide.

Now, of my threescore years and ten,
Twenty will not come again,
And take from seventy springs a score,
It only leaves me fifty more.

And since to look at things in bloom
Fifty springs are little room,
About the woodlands I will go
To see the cherry hung with snow.

A. E. HOUSMAN

[126]

Apple-trees

When autumn stains and dapples
The diverse land,
Thickly studded with apples
The apple-trees stand.

Their mystery none discovers,
So none can tell —
Not the most passionate lovers
Of garth and fell;
For the silent sunlight weaves
The orchard spell,
Bough, bole, and root,
Mysterious, hung with leaves,
Embossed with fruit.

Though merle and throstle were loud,
Silent *their* passion in spring,
A blush of blossom wild-scented;
And now when no song-birds sing,
They are heavy with apples and proud
And supremely contented —
All fertile and green and sappy,
No wish denied,
Exceedingly quiet and happy
And satisfied!

No jealousy, anger, or fashion
Of strife
Perturbs in their stations
The apple-trees. Life
Is an effortless passion,
Fruit, bough, and stem,
A beautiful patience
For them.

Frost of the harvest-moon
Changes their sap to wine;
Ruddy and golden soon
Their clustered orbs will shine,
By favour
Of many a wind,
Of morn and noon and night,
Fulfilled from core to rind
With savour
Of all delight.

JOHN DAVIDSON

The Pines

We sleep in the sleep of ages, the bleak, barbarian pines;
The gray moss drapes us like sages, and closer we lock our lines,
And deeper we clutch through the gelid gloom where never a
   sunbeam shines.

On the flanks of the storm-gored ridges are our black battalions
   massed;
We surge in a host to the sullen coast, and we sing in the ocean
   blast;
From empire of sea to empire of snow we grip our empire fast.

To the niggard lands were we driven, 'twixt desert and floes are
   we penned;
To us was the Northland given, ours to stronghold and defend;
Ours till the world be riven in the crash of the utter end;

Ours from the bleak beginning, through the æons of death-like
   sleep;
Ours from the shock when the naked rock was hurled from the
   hissing deep;
Ours through the twilight ages of weary glacier creep.

[128]

Wind of the East, Wind of the West, wandering to and fro,
Chant your songs in our topmost boughs, that the sons of men
    may know
The peerless pine was the first to come, and the pine will be
    last to go!

We pillar the halls of perfumed gloom; we plume where the
    eagles soar;
The North-wind swoops from the brooding Pole, and our ancients
    crash and roar;
But where one falls from the crumbling walls shoots up a hardy
    score.

We spring from the gloom of the canyon's womb; in the valley's
    lap we lie;
From the white foam-fringe, where the breakers cringe, to the
    peaks that tusk the sky,
We climb, and we peer in the crag-locked mere that gleams like a
    golden eye.

Gain to the verge of the hog-back ridge where the vision ranges
    free:
Pines and pines and the shadow of pines as far as the eye can see;
A steadfast legion of stalwart knights in dominant empery.

Sun, moon and stars give answer; shall we not staunchly stand,
Even as now, forever, wards of the wilder strand,
Sentinels of the stillness, lords of the last, lone land?

ROBERT SERVICE

Verses on the Destruction
of the Woods near Drumlanrig

As on the banks o' wandering Nith,
  Ae smiling simmer-morn I stray'd,
And traced its bonnie howes and haughs,
  Where linties sang and lambkins play'd,
I sat me down upon a craig,
  And drank my fill o' fancy's dream,
When, from the eddying deep below,
  Uprose the genius of the stream.

Dark, like the frowning rock, his brow,
  And troubled, like his wintry wave,
And deep, as soughs the boding wind
  Amang his eaves, the sight he gave —
'And came ye here, my son', he cried,
  'To wander in my birken shade?
To muse some favourite Scottish theme,
  Or sing some favourite Scottish maid?

'There was a time, it's nae lang syne,
  Ye might hae seen me in my pride,
When a' my banks sae bravely saw
  Their woody pictures in my tide;
When hanging beech and spreading elm
  Shaded my stream sae clear and cool,
And stately oaks their twisted arms
  Threw broad and dark across the pool;

'When glinting, through the trees, appear'd
  The wee white cot aboon the mill,
And peacefu' rose its ingle reek,
  That slowly curling clamb the hill.
But now the cot is bare and cauld,
  Its branchy shelter's lost and gane,
And scarce a stinted birk is left
  To shiver in the blast its lane.'

[130]

PLANS AND TREES

'Alas!' quoth I, 'what ruefu' chance
    Has twined ye o' your stately trees?
Has laid your rocky bosom bare?
    Has stripp'd the cleeding o' your braes?
Was it the bitter eastern blast,
    That scatters blight in early spring?
Or was't the wil'fire scorch'd their boughs,
    Or canker-worm wi' secret sting?'

'Nae eastlin blast,' the sprite replied;
    'It blew na here sae fierce and fell,
And on my dry and halesome banks
    Nae canker-worms get leave to dwell:
Man! cruel man!' the genius sigh'd
    As through the cliffs he sank him down —
'The worm that gnaw'd my bonnie trees,
    That reptile wears a ducal crown.'

ROBERT BURNS

Binsey Poplars

felled 1879

My aspens dear, whose airy cages quelled,
Quelled or quenched in leaves the leaping sun,
All felled, felled, are all felled;
    Of a fresh and following folded rank
        Not spared, not one
        That dandled a sandalled
    Shadow that swam or sank
On meadow and river and wind-wandering weed-winding bank.

[131]

O if we but knew what we do
     When we delve or hew —
   Hack and rack the growing green!
    Since country is so tender
To touch, her being so slender,
That, like this sleek and seeing ball
But a prick will make no eye at all,
Where we, even where we mean

    To mend her we end her,
    When we hew or delve:
After-comers cannot guess the beauty been.
   Ten or twelve, only ten or twelve
    Strokes of havoc unselve
     The sweet especial scene,
    Rural scene, a rural scene,
    Sweet especial rural scene.

GERARD MANLEY HOPKINS

Section 3
ANIMALS

Snake

A snake came to my water-trough
On a hot, hot day, and I in pyjamas for the heat,
To drink there.

In the deep, strange-scented shade of the great dark carob-tree
I came down the steps with my pitcher
And must wait, must stand and wait, for there he was at the trough
    before me.

He reached down from a fissure in the earth-wall in the gloom
And trailed his yellow-brown slackness soft-bellied down, over the
    edge of the stone trough
And rested his throat upon the stone bottom,
And where the water had dripped from the tap, in a small
    clearness,
He sipped with his straight mouth,
Softly drank through his straight gums, into his slack long body,
Silently.

Someone was before me at my water-trough,
And I, like a second comer, waiting.

He lifted his head from his drinking, as cattle do,
And looked at me vaguely, as drinking cattle do,
And flickered his two-forked tongue from his lips, and mused
    a moment,
And stooped and drank a little more,
Being earth-brown, earth-golden from the burning bowels of the
    earth
On the day of Sicilian July, with Etna smoking.

The voice of my education said to me
He must be killed,
For in Sicily the black, black snakes are innocent, the gold are
    venomous.

And voices in me said, If you were a man
You would take a stick and break him now, and finish him off.

But must I confess how I liked him,
How glad I was he had come like a guest in quiet, to drink at my
    water-trough
And depart peaceful, pacified, and thankless,
Into the burning bowels of this earth?

Was it cowardice, that I dared not kill him?
Was it perversity, that I longed to talk to him?
Was it humility, to feel so honoured?
I felt so honoured.

And yet those voices:
If you were not afraid, you would kill him!

And truly I was afraid, I was most afraid,
But even so, honoured still more
That he should seek my hospitality
From out the dark door of the secret earth.

He drank enough
And lifted his head, dreamily, as one who has drunken,
And flickered his tongue like a forked night on the air, so black,
Seeming to lick his lips,
And looked around like a god, unseeing, into the air,
And slowly turned his head,
And slowly, very slowly, as if thrice adream,
Proceeded to draw his slow length curving round
And climb again the broken bank of my wall-face.

And as he put his head into that dreadful hole,
And as he slowly drew up, snake-easing his shoulders, and entered
    farther,
A sort of horror, a sort of protest against his withdrawing into that
    horrid black hole,
Deliberately going into the blackness, and slowly drawing himself
    after,
Overcame me now his back was turned.

I looked round, I put down my pitcher,
I picked up a clumsy log
And threw it at the water-trough with a clatter.

I think it did not hit him,
But suddenly that part of him that was left behind convulsed in
    undignified haste,
Writhed like lightning, and was gone
Into the black hole, the earth-lipped fissure in the wall-front,
At which, in the intense still noon, I stared with fascination.

And immediately I regretted it.
I thought how paltry, how vulgar, what a mean act!
I despised myself and the voices of my accursed human education.

And I thought of the albatross,
And I wished he would come back, my snake.

For he seemed to me again like a king,
Like a king in exile, uncrowned in the underworld,
Now due to be crowned again.

And so, I missed my chance with one of the lords
Of life.
And I have something to expiate;
A pettiness.

D. H. LAWRENCE

Baby Tortoise

You know what it is to be born alone,
Baby tortoise!

The first day to heave your feet little by little from the shell,
Not yet awake,
And remain lapsed on earth,
Not quite alive.

ANIMALS

A tiny fragile, half-animate bean.

To open your tiny beak-mouth, that looks as if it would never open,
Like some iron door;
To lift the upper hawk-beak from the lower base
And reach your skinny little neck
And take your first bite at some dim bit of herbage,
Alone, small insect,
Tiny bright-eye,
Slow one.

To take your first solitary bite
And move on your slow, solitary hunt.
Your bright, dark little eye,
Your eye of a dark disturbed night,
Under its slow lid, tiny baby tortoise,
So indomitable.

No one ever heard you complain.

You draw your head forward, slowly, from your little wimple
And set forward, slow-dragging, on your four-pinned toes,
Rowing slowly forward.
Whither away, small bird?
Rather like a baby working its limbs,
Except that you make slow, ageless progress
And a baby makes none.

The touch of sun excites you,
And the long ages, and the lingering chill
Make you pause to yawn,
Opening your impervious mouth,
Suddenly beak-shaped, and very wide, like some suddenly gaping
    pincers;
Soft red tongue, and hard thin gums,
Then close the wedge of your little mountain front,
Your face, baby tortoise.

Do you wonder at the world, as slowly you turn your head in its
   wimple
And look with laconic, black eyes?
Or is sleep coming over you again,
The non-life?

You are so hard to wake.

Are you able to wonder?
Or is it just your indomitable will and pride of the first life
Looking round .
And slowly pitching itself against the inertia
Which had seemed invincible?

The vast inanimate,
And the fine brilliance of your so tiny eye,
Challenger.

Nay, tiny shell-bird,
What a huge vast inanimate it is, that you must row against,
What an incalculable inertia.

Challenger,
Little Ulysses, fore-runner,
No bigger than my thumb-nail,
Buon viaggio.

All animate creation on your shoulder,
Set forth, little Titan, under your battle-shield.

The ponderous, preponderate,
Inanimate universe;
And you are slowly moving, pioneer, you alone.

How vivid your travelling seems now, in the troubled sunshine,
Stoic, Ulyssean atom;
Suddenly hasty, reckless, on high toes.

Voiceless little bird,
Resting your head half out of your wimple
In the slow dignity of your eternal pause.
Alone, with no sense of being alone,
And hence six times more solitary;
Fulfilled of the slow passion of pitching through immemorial ages
Your little round house in the midst of chaos.

Over the garden earth,
Small bird,
Over the edge of all things.

Traveller,
With your tail tucked a little on one side
Like a gentleman in a long-skirted coat.

All life carried on your shoulder,
Invincible fore-runner.

D. H. LAWRENCE

To a Mouse,
on Turning Her Up in her Nest
with the Plough, November 1785

Wee, sleekit, cow'rin, tim'rous beastie,
O what a panic's in thy breastie!
Thou need na start awa sae hasty,
    Wi' bickering brattle!
I wad be laith to rin an' chase thee
    Wi' murd'ring pattle!

I'm truly sorry man's dominion
Has broken Nature's social union,
An' justifies that ill opinion
    Which makes thee startle
At me, thy poor earth-born companion,
    An' fellow-mortal!

[140]

I doubt na, whiles, but thou may thieve;
What then? poor beastie, thou maun live!
A daimen-icker in a thrave
        'S a sma' request:
I'll get a blessin' wi' the lave,
        And never miss't!

Thy wee bit housie, too, in ruin!
Its silly wa's the win's are strewin'!
An' naething, now, to big a new ane,
        O' foggage green!
An' bleak December's winds ensuin',
        Baith snell an' keen!

Thou saw the fields laid bare and waste.
An' weary winter comin' fast,
An' cozie here, beneath the blast,
        Thou thought to dwell,
Till crash! the cruel coulter past
        Out-thro' thy cell.

That wee bit heap o' leaves an' stibble
Has cost thee mony a weary nibble!
Now thou's turn'd out, for a' thy trouble,
        But house or hald,
To thole the winter's sleety dribble,
        An' cranreuch cauld!

But, Mousie, thou art no thy lane,
In proving foresight may be vain:
The best laid schemes o' mice an' men
        Gang aft a-gley,
An' lea'e us nought but grief an' pain
        For promis'd joy.

Still thou art blest compar'd wi' me!
The present only toucheth thee:
But oh! I backward cast my e'e
        On prospects drear!
An' forward tho' I canna see,
        I guess an' fear!

ROBERT BURNS

[141]

Mouse's Nest

I found a ball of grass among the hay
And progged it as I passed and went away;
And when I looked I fancied something stirred,
And turned agen and hoped to catch the bird —
When out an old mouse bolted in the wheats
With all her young ones hanging at her teats;
She looked so odd and so grotesque to me,
I ran and wondered what the thing could be,
And pushed the knapweed bunches where I stood;
Then the mouse hurried from the craking brood.
The young ones squeaked, and as I went away
She found her nest again among the hay.
The water o'er the pebbles scarce could run
And broad old cesspools glittered in the sun.

JOHN CLARE

Hares at Play

The birds are gone to bed the cows are still
And sheep lie panting on each old mole hill
And underneath the willows grey-green bough
Like toil a resting — lies the fallow plough
The timid hares throw daylights fears away
On the lanes road to dust and dance and play
Then dabble in the grain by nought deterred
To lick the dewfall from the barleys beard
Then out they sturt again and round the hill
Like happy thoughts dance squat and loiter still
Till milking maidens in the early morn
Gingle their yokes and start them in the corn
Through well known beaten paths each nimbling hare
Sturts quick as fear — and seeks its hidden lair

JOHN CLARE

On seeing
a Wounded Hare limp by me

Which a fellow had just shot at

Inhuman man! curse on thy barb'rous art,
    And blasted be thy murder-aiming eye;
    May never pity soothe thee with a sigh,
Nor ever pleasure glad thy cruel heart!

Go, live, poor wanderer of the wood and field,
    The bitter little that of life remains;
    No more the thickening brakes and verdant plains
To thee shall home, or food, or pastime yield.

Seek, mangled wretch, some place of wonted rest,
    No more of rest, but now thy dying bed!
    The sheltering rushes whistling o'er thy head,
The cold earth with thy bloody bosom prest.

Perhaps a mother's anguish adds its woe;
  The playful pair crowd fondly be thy side:
  Ah, helpless nurslings! who will now provide
That life a mother only can bestow?

Oft, as by winding Nith, I, musing, wait
  The sober eve, or hail the cheerful dawn,
  I'll miss thee sporting o'er the dewy lawn,
And curse the ruffian's aim, and mourn thy hapless fate.

ROBERT BURNS

Hedgehog

Twitching the leaves just where the drainpipe clogs
In ivy leaves and mud, a purposeful
Creature at night about its business. Dogs
Fear his stiff seriousness. He chews away

At beetles, worms, slugs, frogs. Can kill a hen
With one snap of his jaws, can taunt a snake
To death on muscled spines. Old countrymen
Tell tales of hedgehogs sucking a cow dry.

But this one, cramped by houses, fences, walls,
Must have slept here all winter in that heap
Of compost, or have inched by intervals
Through tidy gardens to this ivy bed.

And here, dim-eyed, but ears so sensitive
A voice within the house can make him freeze.
He scuffs the edge of danger; yet can live
Happily in our nights and absences.

A country creature, wary, quiet and shrewd,
He takes the milk we give him, when we're gone.
At night, our slamming voices must seem crude
To one who sits and waits for silences.

ANTHONY THWAITE

[144]

The Fallow Deer
at the Lonely House

One without looks in to-night
  Through the curtain-chink
From the sheet of glistening white;
One without looks in to-night
  As we sit and think
  By the fender-brink.

We do not discern those eyes
  Watching in the snow;
Lit by lamps of rosy dyes
We do not discern those eyes
  Wondering, aglow,
  Fourfooted, tiptoe.

THOMAS HARDY

The Fox at the Point of Death

A fox, in life's extream decay,
Weak, sick and faint, expiring lay;
All appetite had left his maw,
And age disarmed his mumbling jaw.
His num'rous race around him stand
To learn their dying sire's command;
He raised his head with whining moan,
And thus was heard the feeble tone.
  Ah sons, from evil ways depart,
My crimes lye heavy on my heart.
See, see, the murdered geese appear!
Why are those bleeding turkeys there?
Why all around this cackling train,
Who haunt my ears for chicken slain?

[145]

ANIMALS

The hungry foxes round them stared,
And for the promised feast prepared.
    Where, Sir, is all this dainty cheer?
Nor turkey, goose, nor hen is here.
These are the phantoms of your brain,
And your sons lick their lips in vain.
    O gluttons, says the drooping sire;
Restrain inordinate desire;
Your liqu'rish taste you shall deplore,
When peace of conscience is no more.
Does not the hound betray our pace,
And gins and guns destroy our race?
Thieves dread the searching eye of power,
And never feel the quiet hour.
Old age (which few of us shall know)
Now puts a period to my woe.
Would you true happiness attain,
Let honesty your passions rein;
So live in credit and esteem,
And, the good name you lost, redeem.
    The counsel's good, a fox replies,
Could we perform what you advise.
Think, what our ancestors have done;
A line of thieves from son to son:
To us descends the long disgrace,
And infamy hath marked our race.
Though we, like harmless sheep, should feed,
Honest in thought, in word, and deed,
Whatever hen-roost is decreased,
We shall be thought to share the feast.
The change shall never be believed,
A lost good-name is ne'er retrived.
    Nay then, replys the feeble Fox,
(But hark! I hear a hen that clocks)
Go, but be mod'rate in your food;
A chicken too might do me good.

JOHN GAY

[146]

The Vixen

Among the taller wood with ivy hung,
The old fox plays and dances round her young.
She snuffs and barks if any passes by
And swings her tail and turns prepared to fly.
The horseman hurries by, she bolts to see,
And turns agen, from danger never free.
If any stands she runs among the poles
And barks and snaps and drives them in the holes.
The shepherd sees them and the boy goes by
And gets a stick and progs the hole to try.
They get all still and lie in safety sure,
And out again when everything's secure,
And start and snap at blackbirds bouncing by
To fight and catch the great white butterfly.

JOHN CLARE

Young Reynard

I

Gracefullest leaper, the dappled fox-cub
  Curves over brambles with berries and buds,
Light as a bubble that flies from the tub,
  Whisked by the laundry-wife out of her suds.
Wavy he comes, woolly, all at his ease,
Elegant, fashioned to foot with the deuce;
Nature's own prince of the dance: then he sees
  Me, and retires as if making excuse.

II

Never closed minuet courtlier! Soon
  Cub-hunting troops were abroad, and a yelp
Told of sure scent: ere the stroke upon noon
  Reynard the younger lay far beyond help.
Wild, my poor friend, has the fate to be chased;
  Civil will conquer: were t'other t'were worse;
Fair, by the flushed early morning embraced,
Haply you live a day longer in verse.

GEORGE MEREDITH

The Badger

The badger grunting on his woodland track
With shaggy hide and sharp nose scrowed with black
Roots in the bushes and the woods and makes
A great huge burrow in the ferns and brakes
With nose on ground he runs an awkward pace
And anything will beat him in the race
The shepherd's dog will run him to his den
Followed and hooted by the dogs and men
The woodman when the hunting comes about
Goes round at night to stop the foxes out
And hurrying through the bushes ferns and brakes
Nor sees the many holes the badger makes

[148]

ANIMALS

And often through the bushes to the chin
Breaks the old holes and tumbles headlong in.

When midnight comes a host of dogs and men
Go out and track the badger to his den
And put a sack within the hole and lie
Till the old grunting badger passes by
He comes and hears them let the strongest loose
The old fox hears the noise and drops the goose
The poacher shoots and hurries from the cry
And the old hare half wounded buzzes by
They get a forked stick to bear him down
And clap the dogs and bear him to the town
And bait him all the day with many dogs
And laugh and shout and fright the scampering hogs
He runs along and bites at all he meets
They shout and hollo down the noisy streets.

He turns about to face the loud uproar
And drives the rebels to their very door
The frequent stone is hurled where ere they go
When badgers fight and every one's a foe
The dogs are clapped and urged to join the fray
The badger turns and drives them all away
Though scarcely half as big dimute and small
He fights with dogs for hours and beats them all
The heavy mastiff savage in the fray
Lies down and licks his feet and turns away
The bulldog knows his match and waxes cold
The badger grins and never leaves his hold
He drives the crowd and follows at their heels
And bites them though the drunkard swears and reels.

The frightened women take the boys away
The blackguard laughs and hurries on the fray
He tries to reach the woods an awkward race
But sticks and cudgels quickly stop the chase
He turns again and drives the noisy crowd
And beats the many dogs in noises loud
He drives away and beats them every one
And then they loose them all and set them on

[149]

ANIMALS

He falls as dead and kicked by boys and men
Then starts and grins and drives the crowd again
Till kicked and torn and beaten out he lies
And leaves his hold and cackles groans and dies.

Some keep a baited badger tame as hog
And tame him till he follows like the dog
They urge him on like dogs and show fair play
He beats and scarcely wounded goes away
Lapped up as if asleep he scorns to fly
And seizes any dog that ventures nigh
Clapped like a dog he never bites the men
But worries dogs and hurries to his den
They let him out and turn a harrow down
And there he fights the host of all the town
He licks the patting hand and tries to play
And never tries to bite or run away
And runs away from noise in hollow trees
Burnt by the boys to get a swarm of bees.

JOHN CLARE

Pumas

Hushed, cruel, amber-eyed,
Before the time of the danger of the day,
Or at dusk on the boulder-broken mountainside
  The great cats seek their prey.

Soft-padded, heavy-limbed,
With agate talons chiselled for love or hate,
In desolate places wooded or granite-rimmed,
  The great cats seek their mate.

Rippling, as water swerved,
To tangled coverts overshadowed and deep
Or secret caves where the canyon's wall is curved,
  The great cats go for sleep.

Seeking the mate or prey,
Out of the darkness glow the insatiate eyes.
Man, who is made more terrible far than they,
  Dreams he is otherwise!

GEORGE STERLING

Mountain Lion

Climbing through the January snow, into the Lobo canyon
Dark grow the spruce-trees, blue is the balsam, water sounds still
  unfrozen, and the trail is still evident.

Men!
Two men!
Men! The only animal in the world to fear!

ANIMALS

They hesitate.
We hesitate.
They have a gun.
We have no gun.

Then we all advance, to meet.

Two Mexicans, strangers, emerging out of the dark and snow and
  inwardness of the Lobo valley.
What are they doing here on this vanishing trail?

What is he carrying?
Something yellow.
A deer?
Què tiene, amigo?
León —

He smiles, foolishly, as if he were caught doing wrong.
And we smile, foolishly, as if we didn't know.
He is quite gentle and dark-faced.

It is a mountain lion,
A long, long slim cat, yellow like a lioness.
Dead.
He trapped her this morning, he says, smiling foolishly.

Lift up her face,
Her round, bright face, bright as frost.
Her round, fine-fashioned head, with two dead ears;
And stripes in the brilliant frost of her face, sharp, fine dark rays.
Dark, keen, fine rays in the brilliant frost of her face.
Beautiful dead eyes.

Hermoso es!

[152]

They go out towards the open;
We go on into the gloom of Lobo.
And above the trees I found her lair,
A hole in the blood-orange brilliant rocks that stick up, a little
    cave.
And bones, and twigs, and a perilous ascent.

So, she will never leap up that way again, with the yellow flash of a
    mountain lion's long shoot!
And her bright striped frost-face will never watch any more, out of
    the shadow of the cave in the blood-orange rock,
Above the trees of the Lobo dark valley-mouth!

Instead, I look out.
And out to the dim of the desert, like a dream, never real;
To the snow of the Sangre de Cristo mountains, the ice of the
    mountains of Picoris,
And near across at the opposite steep of snow, green trees
    motionless standing in snow, like a Christmas toy.

And I think in this empty world there was room for me and a
    mountain lion.
And I think in the world beyond, how easily we might spare a
    million or two of humans
And never miss them.
Yet what a gap in the world, the missing white frost-face of that
    slim yellow mountain lion!

                                        D. H. LAWRENCE

[153]

Kangaroo

In the northern hemisphere
Life seems to leap at the air, or skim under the wind
Like stags on rocky ground, or pawing horses, or springy
    scut-tailed rabbits.

Or else rush horizontal to charge at the sky's horizon,
Like bulls or bisons or wild pigs.

Or slip like water slippery towards its ends,
As foxes, stoats, and wolves, and prairie dogs.

ANIMALS

Only mice, and moles, and rats, and badgers, and beavers, and
   perhaps bears
Seem belly-plumbed to the earth's mid-navel.
Or frogs that when they leap come flop, and flop to the centre of
   the earth.

But the yellow antipodal Kangaroo, when she sits up,
Who can unseat her, like a liquid drop that is heavy, and just
   touches earth.

The downward drip
The down-urge.
So much denser than cold-blooded frogs.

Delicate mother Kangaroo
Sitting up there rabbit-wise, but huge, plumb-weighted,
And lifting her beautiful slender face, oh! so much more gently and
   finely lined than a rabbit's, or than a hare's,
Lifting her face to nibble at a round white peppermint drop, which
   she loves, sensitive mother Kangaroo.

Her sensitive, long, pure-bred face.
Her full antipodal eyes, so dark,
So big and quiet and remote, having watched so many empty
   dawns in silent Australia.

Her little loose hands, and drooping Victorian shoulders.
And then her great weight below the waist, her vast pale belly
With a thin young yellow little paw hanging out, and straggle of a
   long thin ear, like ribbon,
Like a funny trimming to the middle of her belly, thin little dangle
   of an immature paw, and one thin ear.

Her belly, her big haunches
And, in addition, the great muscular python-stretch of her tail.

There, she shan't have any more peppermint drops.
So she wistfully, sensitively sniffs the air, and then turns, goes off in
   slow sad leaps

[155]

On the long flat skis of her legs,
Steered and propelled by that steel-strong snake of a tail.

Stops again, half turns, inquisitive to look back.
While something stirs quickly in her belly, and a lean little face
    comes out, as from a window,
Peaked and a bit dismayed,
Only to disappear again quickly away from the sight of the world,
    to snuggle down in the warmth,
Leaving the trail of a different paw hanging out.

Still she watches with eternal, cocked wistfulness!
How full her eyes are, like the full, fathomless, shining eyes of an
    Australian black-boy
Who has been lost so many centuries on the margins of existence!

She watches with insatiable wistfulness.
Untold centuries of watching for something to come,
For a new signal from life, in that silent lost land of the South.

Where nothing bites but insects and snakes and the sun, small life.
Where no bull roared, no cow ever lowed, no stag cried, no
    leopard screeched, no lion coughed, no dog barked,
But all was silent save for parrots occasionally, in the haunted blue
    bush.

Wistfully watching, with wonderful liquid eyes.
And all her weight, all her blood, dripping sack-wise down towards
    the earth's centre,
And the live little-one taking in its paw at the door of her belly.

Leap then, and come down on the line that draws to the earth's
    deep, heavy centre.

D. H. LAWRENCE

The Elephant is Slow to Mate

The elephant, the huge old beast,
　　　is slow to mate;
he finds a female, they show no haste
　　　they wait

for the sympathy in their vast shy hearts
　　　slowly, slowly to rouse
as they loiter along the river-beds
　　　and drink and browse

and dash in panic through the brake
　　　of forest with the herd,
and sleep in massive silence, and wake
　　　together, without a word.

So slowly the great hot elephant hearts
　　　grow full of desire,
and the great beasts mate in secret at last,
　　　hiding their fire.

Oldest they are and the wisest of beasts
　　　so they know at last
how to wait for the loneliest of feasts
　　　for the full repast.

They do not snatch, they do not tear;
　　　their massive blood
moves as the moon-tides, near, more near,
　　　till they touch in flood.

D. H. LAWRENCE

from

Song of Myself

I think I could turn and live with animals, they are so placid and
   self-contained;
I stand and look at them long and long.
They do not sweat and whine about their condition;
They do not lie awake in the dark and weep for their sins;
They do not make me sick discussing their duty to God;
Not one is dissastisfied — not one is demented with the mania of
   owning things;
Not one kneels to another, nor to his kind that lived thousands of
   years ago;
Not one is respectable or industrious over the whole earth.

WALT WHITMAN

Section 4

INSECTS
AND SMALL CREATURES

The Grasshopper

O thou that swing'st upon the waving hair
    Of some well-fillèd oaten beard,
Drunk every night with a delicious tear
    Dropt thee from heaven, where thou wert rear'd!

The joys of earth and air are thine entire,
    That with thy feet and wings dost hop and fly;
And when thy poppy works, thou dost retire
    To thy carved acorn-bed to lie.

Up with the day, the Sun thou welcom'st then,
    Sport'st in the gilt plaits of his beams,
And all these merry days mak'st merry men,
    Thyself, and melancholy streams.

RICHARD LOVELACE

On the Grasshopper and Cricket

The poetry of earth is never dead:
　　When all the birds are faint with the hot sun,
　　And hide in cooling trees, a voice will run
From hedge to hedge about the new-mown mead:
That is the grasshopper's — he takes the lead
　　In summer luxury, — he has never done
　　With his delights, for when tired out with fun,
He rests at ease beneath some pleasant weed.
The poetry of earth is ceasing never:
　　On a lone winter evening, when the frost
Has wrought a silence, from the stove there shrills
The Cricket's song, in warmth increasing ever,
　　And seems to one in drowsiness half lost,
The Grasshopper's among some grassy hills.

JOHN KEATS

To the Grasshopper and the Cricket

Green little vaulter in the sunny grass
Catching your heart up at the feel of June,
Sole voice that's heard amidst the lazy noon,
When ev'n the bees lag at the summoning brass;
And you, warm little housekeeper, who class
With those who think the candles come too soon,
Loving the fire, and with your tricksome tune
Nick the glad silent moments as they pass;
Oh sweet and tiny cousins, that belong,
One to the fields, the other to the hearth,
Both have your sunshine; both though small are strong
At your clear hearts; and both were sent on earth
To sing in thoughtful ears this natural song, —
In doors and out, summer and winter, Mirth.

LEIGH HUNT

[162]

Clock-a-clay

In the cowslip pips I lie
Hidden from the buzzing fly,
While green grass beneath me lies
Pearled wi' dew like fishes' eyes.
Here I lie, a clock-a-clay,
Waiting for the time of day.

While grassy forests quake surprise,
And the wild wind sobs and sighs,
My gold home rocks as like to fall
On its pillar green and tall;
When the pattering rain drives by
Clock-a-clay keeps warm and dry.

Day by day and night by night
All the week I hide from sight.
In the cowslip pips I lie,
In rain and dew still warm and dry.
Day and night, and night and day,
Red, black-spotted clock-a-clay.

My home it shakes in wind and showers,
Pale green pillar topped wi' flowers,
Bending at the wild wind's breath
Till I touch the grass beneath.
Here I live, lone clock-a-clay,
Watching for the time of day.

JOHN CLARE

Lines to a Dragon Fly

Life (priest and poet say) is but a dream;
    I wish no happier one than to be laid
    Beneath some cool syringa's scented shade
Or wavy willow, by the running stream,
    Brimful of Moral, where the Dragon Fly,
    Wanders as careless and content as I.
Thanks for this fancy, insect king,
Of purple crest and filmy wing,
Who with indifference givest up
The water-lily's golden cup,
To come again and overlook
What I am writing in my book.
Believe me, most who read the line
Will read with hornier eyes than thine;
And yet their souls shall live for ever,
And thine drop dead into the river!
God pardon them, O insect king,
Who fancy so unjust a thing!

WALTER SAVAGE LANDOR

The Ant-heap

High in the woodland, on the mountain-side,
    I ponder, half a golden afternoon,
Storing deep strength to battle with the tide
    I must encounter soon.

Absorbed, inquisitive, alert, irate,
    The wiry wood-ants run beneath the pines,
And bustle if a careless footfall grate
    Among their travelled lines.

With prey unwieldy, slain in alien lands,
  When shadows fall aslant, laden they come,
Where, piled of red fir-needles, guarded stands
  Their dry and rustling dome.

They toil for what they know not; rest they shun;
  They nip the soft intruder; when they die
They grapple pain and fate, and ask from none
  The pity they deny.

A. C. BENSON

Upon the Snail

She goes but softly, but she goeth sure;
  She stumbles not as stronger creatures do:
Her journey's shorter, so she may endure
  Better than they which do much further go.

She makes no noise, but stilly seizeth on
  The flower or herb appointed for her food,
The which she quietly doth feed upon,
  While others range, and gare, but find no good.

And though she doth but very softly go,
  However 'tis not fast, nor slow, but sure;
And certainly they that do travel so,
  The prize they do aim at they do procure.

JOHN BUNYAN

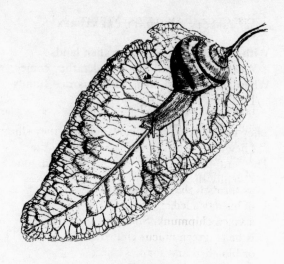

The Snail

All day shut fast in whorled retreat
You slumber where — no wild bird knows;
While on your rounded roof-tree beat
The petals of the rose.
The grasses sigh above your house;
Through drifts of darkest azure sweep
The sun-motes where the mosses drowse
That soothe your noonday sleep.

But when to ashes in the west
Those sun-fires die; and, silver, slim,
Eve, with the moon upon her breast,
Smiles on the uplands dim;
Then, all your wreathèd house astir,
Horns reared, grim mouth, deliberate pace,
You glide in silken silence where
The feast awaits your grace.

Strange partners, Snail! Then I, abed,
Consign the thick-darked vault to you,
Nor heed what sweetness night may shed
Nor moonshine's slumbrous dew.

WALTER DE LA MARE

[166]

Slug in Woods

For eyes he waves greentipped
taut horns of slime. They dipped,
hours back, across a reef,
a salmonberry leaf.
Then strained to grope past fin
of spruce. Now eyes suck in
as through the hemlock butts
of his day's ledge there cuts
a vixen chipmunk. Stilled
is he — green mucus chilled,
or blotched and soapy stone,
pinguid in moss, alone.
Hours on, he will resume
his silver scrawl, illume
his palimpsest, emboss
his diver's line across
that waving green illim-
itable seafloor. Slim
young jay his sudden shark;
the wrecks he skirts are dark
and fungussed firlogs, whom
spirea sprays emplume,
encoral. Dew his shell,
while mounting boles foretell
of isles in dappled air
fathoms above his care.
Azygous muted life,
himself his viscid wife,
foodward he noses cold beneath his sea.
So spends a summer's jasper century.

EARLE BIRNEY

The Study of a Spider

From holy flower to holy flower
Thou weavest thine unhallowed bower.
The harmless dewdrops, beaded thin,
Ripple along thy ropes of sin.
Thy house a grave, a gulf thy throne
Affright the fairies every one.
Thy winding sheets are grey and fell,
Imprisoning with nets of hell
The lovely births that winnow by,
Winged sisters of the rainbow sky:
Elf-darlings, fluffy, bee-bright things,
And owl-white moths with mealy wings,
And tiny flies, as gauzy thin
As e'er were shut electrum in.
These are thy death spoils, insect ghoul,
With their dear life thy fangs are foul.
Thou felon anchorite of pain
Who sittest in a world of slain.
Hermit, who tunest song unsweet
To heaving wing and writhing feet.
A glutton of creation's sighs,
Miser of many miseries.

Toper, whose lonely feasting chair
Sways in inhospitable air.
The board is bare, the bloated host
Drinks to himself toast after toast.
His lip requires no goblet brink,
But like a weasel must he drink.
The vintage is as old as time
And bright as sunset, pressed and prime.
Ah venom mouth and shaggy thighs
And paunch grown sleek with sacrifice,
Thy dolphin back and shoulders round
Coarse-hairy as some goblin hound
Whom a hag rides to sabbath on,
While shuddering stars in fear grow wan.

[168]

Thou palace priest of treachery,
Thou type of selfish lechery,
I break the toils around thy head
And from their gibbets take thy dead.

JOHN LEICESTER WARREN,
LORD DE TABLEY

The Humble-bee

Burly, dozing humble-bee,
Where thou art is clime for me.
Let them sail for Porto Rique,
Far-off heats through seas to seek;
I will follow thee alone,
Thou animated torrid-zone!
Zigzag steerer, desert cheerer,
Let me chase thy waving lines;
Keep me nearer, me thy hearer,
Singing over shrubs and vines.

Insect lover of the sun,
Joy of thy dominion!
Sailor of the atmosphere;
Swimmer through the waves of air;
Voyager of light and noon;
Epicurean of June;
Wait, I prithee, till I come
Within earshot of thy hum, —
All without is martyrdom.

When the south wind, in May days,
With a net of shining haze
Silvers the horizon wall,
And with softness touching all,
Tints the human countenance
With a color of romance,
And infusing subtle heats,
Turns the sod to violets,

Thou, in sunny solitudes,
Rover of the underwoods,
The green silence dost displace
With thy mellow, breezy bass.

Hot midsummer's petted crone,
Sweet to me thy drowsy tone
Tells of countless sunny hours,
Long days, and solid banks of flowers;
Of gulfs of sweetness without bound
In Indian wildernesses found;
Of Syrian peace, immortal leisure,
Firmest cheer, and bird-like pleasure.

Aught unsavory or unclean
Hath my insect never seen;
But violets and bilberry bells,
Maple-sap and daffodels,
Grass with green flag half-mast high,
Succory to match the sky,
Columbine with horn of honey,
Scented fern, and agrimony,
Clover, catchfly, adder's-tongue
And brier-roses, dwelt among;
All beside was unknown waste,
All was picture as he passed.

Wiser far than human seer,
Yellow-breeched philosopher!
Seeing only what is fair,
Sipping only what is sweet,
Thou dost mock at fate and care,
Leave the chaff, and take the wheat.
When the fierce northwestern blast
Cools sea and land so far and fast,
Thou already slumberest deep;
Woe and want thou canst outsleep;
Want and woe, which torture us,
Thy sleep makes ridiculous.

RALPH WALDO EMERSON

[170]

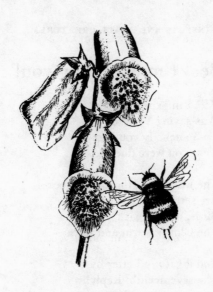

The Bee

Like trains of cars on tracks of plush
I hear the level bee:
A jar across the flowers goes,
Their velvet masonry

Withstands until the sweet assault
Their chivalry consumes,
While he, victorious, tilts away
To vanquish other blooms.

His feet are shod with gauze,
His helmet is of gold;
His breast, a single onyx
With chrysoprase, inlaid.

His labor is a chant,
His idleness a tune;
Oh, for a bee's experience
Of clovers and of noon!

EMILY DICKINSON

[171]

'Bee! I'm expecting you!'

Bee! I'm expecting you!
Was saying Yesterday
To Somebody you know
That you were due —

The Frogs got Home last Week —
Are settled, and at work —
Birds, mostly back —
The Clover warm and thick —

You'll get my Letter by
The seventeenth; Reply
Or better, be with me —
Yours, Fly.

EMILY DICKINSON

Mosquito

When did you start your tricks,
Monsieur?

What do you stand on such high legs for?
Why this length of shredded shank,
You exaltation?

Is it so that you shall lift your centre of gravity upwards
And weigh no more than air as you alight upon me,
Stand upon me weightless, you phantom?

I heard a woman call you the Winged Victory
In sluggish Venice.
You turn your head towards your tail, and smile.

[172]

How can you put so much devilry
Into that translucent phantom shred
Of a frail corpus?

Queer, with your thin wings and your streaming legs,
How you sail like a heron, or a dull clot of air,
A nothingness.

Yet what an aura surrounds you;
Your evil little aura, prowling, and casting a numbness on
    my mind.

That is your trick, your bit of filthy magic:
Invisibility, and the anæsthetic power
To deaden my attention in your direction.

But I know your game now, streaky sorcerer.
Queer, how you stalk and prowl the air
In circles and evasions, enveloping me,
Ghoul on wings
Winged Victory.

Settle, and stand on long thin shanks
Eyeing me sideways, and cunningly conscious that I am aware,
You speck.

I hate the way you lurch off sideways into air
Having read my thoughts against you.

Come then, let us play at unawares,
And see who wins in this sly game of bluff.
Man or mosquito.

You don't know that I exist, and I don't know that you exist.
Now then!

It is your trump,
It is your hateful little trump,
You pointed fiend,
Which shakes my sudden blood to hatred of you:
It is your small, high, hateful bugle in my ear.

[173]

Why do you do it?
Surely it is bad policy.

They say you can't help it.

If that is so, then I believe a little in Providence protecting the
    innocent.
But it sounds so amazingly like a slogan,
A yell of triumph as you snatch my scalp.

Blood, red blood
Super-magical
Forbidden liquor.

I behold you stand
For a second enspasmed in oblivion.
Obscenely ecstasied
Sucking live blood,
My blood.

Such silence, such suspended transport,
Such gorging,
Such obscenity of trespass.

You stagger
As well as you may.
Only your accursed hairy frailty,
Your own imponderable weightlessness
Saves you, wafts you away on the very draught my anger makes in
    its snatching.

Away with a pæan of derision,
You winged blood-drop.

Can I not overtake you?
Are you one too many for me,
Winged Victory?
Am I not mosquito enough to out-mosquito you?

[174]

Queer, what a big stain my sucked blood makes
Beside the infinitesimal faint smear of you!
Queer, what a dim dark smudge you have disappeared into!

D. H. LAWRENCE

Butterfly

Butterfly, the wind blows sea-ward, strong beyond the garden wall!
Butterfly, why do you settle on my shoe, and sip the dirt on my
   shoe,
lifting your veined wings, lifting them? big white butterfly!

Already it is October, and the wind blows strong to the sea
from the hills where snow must have fallen, the wind is polished
   with snow.

Here in the garden, with red geraniums, it is warm, it is warm
but the wind blows strong to sea-ward, white butterfly, content on
   my shoe!

Will you go, will you go from my warm house?
Will you climb on your big soft wings, black-dotted,
as up an invisible rainbow, an arch
till the wind slides you sheer from the arch-crest
and in a strange level fluttering you go out to sea-ward white speck!

Farewell, farewell, lost soul!
you have melted in the crystalline distance,
it is enough! I saw you vanish into air.

D. H. LAWRENCE

Insects

These tiny loiterers on the barley's beard,
And happy units of a numerous herd
Of playfellows, the laughing summer brings,
Mocking the sunshine in their glittering wings,
How merrily they creep, and run, and fly!
No kin they bear to labour's drudgery,
Smoothing the velvet of the pale hedge-rose;
And where they fly for dinner no one knows —
The dew-drops feed them not — they love the shine
Of noon, whose sun may bring them golden wine.
All day they're playing in their Sunday dress —
Till night goes sleep, and they can do no less;
Then, to the heath-bell's silken hood they fly,
And like to princes in their slumbers lie,
Secure from night, and dropping dews, and all,
In silken beds and roomy painted hall.
So merrily they spend their summer day,
Now in the cornfields, now the new-mown hay,
One almost fancies that such happy things,
With coloured hoods and richly burnished wings,

[176]

Are fairy folk, in splendid masquerade
Disguised, as if of mortal folk afraid,
Keeping their merry pranks a mystery still,
Lest glaring day should do their secrets ill.

JOHN CLARE

An August Midnight

A shaded lamp and a waving blind,
And the beat of a clock from a distant floor;
On this scene enter — winged, horned, and spined —
A longlegs, a moth, and a dumbledore;
While 'mid my page there idly stands
A sleepy fly, that rubs its hands . . .

Thus meet we five, in this still place,
At this point of time, at this point in space.
— My guests besmear my new-penned line,
Or bang at the lamp, and fall supine.
'God's humblest, they!' I muse. Yet why?
They know Earth-secrets that know not I.

THOMAS HARDY

Section 5
SEASONS

from

The Seasons — Spring

When first the Soul of Love is sent abroad,
Warm thro' the vital Air, and on the Heart
Harmonious seizes, the gay Troops begin,
In gallant Thought, to plume the painted Wing;
And try again the long-forgotten Strain,
At first faint-warbled. But no sooner grows
The soft Infusion prevalent, and wide,
Than, all alive, at once their Joy o'erflows
In Musick unconfin'd. Up-springs the Lark,
Shrill-voic'd, and loud, the Messenger of Morn;
Ere yet the Shadows fly, he mounted sings
Amid the dawning Clouds, and from their Haunts
Calls up the tuneful Nations. Every Copse
Deep-tangled, Tree irregular, and Bush
Bending with dewy Moisture, o'er the Heads
Of the coy Quiristers that lodge within,
Are prodigal of Harmony. The Thrush
And Wood-lark, o'er the kind contending Throng
Superior heard, run thro' the sweetest Length
Of Notes; when listening *Philomela* deigns
To let them joy, and purposes, in Thought
Elate, to make her Night excel their Day.
The Black-bird whistles from the thorny Brake;
The mellow Bullfinch answers from the Grove:
Nor are the Linnets, o'er the flowering Furze
Pour'd out profusely, silent. Join'd to These,
Innumerous Songsters, in the freshening Shade
Of new-sprung Leaves, their Modulations mix
Mellifluous. The Jay, the Rook, the Daw,
And each harsh Pipe, discordant heard alone,
Aid the full Concert: while the Stock-dove breathes
A melancholy Murmur thro' the Whole.

'Tis Love creates their Melody, and all
This Waste of Music is the Voice of Love;
That even to Birds, and Beasts, the tender Arts
Of pleasing teaches. Hence the glossy Kind
Try every winning Way inventive Love
Can dictate, and in Courtship to their Mates
Pour forth their little Souls. First, wide around,
With distant Awe, in airy Rings they rove,
Endeavouring by a thousand Tricks to catch
The cunning, conscious, half-averted Glance
Of their regardless Charmer. Should she seem
Softening the least Approvance to bestow,
Their Colours burnish, and by Hope inspir'd,
They brisk advance; then, on a sudden struck,
Retire disorder'd; then again approach;
In fond Rotation spread the spotted Wing,
And shiver every Feather with Desire.

   Connubial Leagues agreed, to the deep Woods
They haste away, all as their Fancy leads,
Pleasure, or Food, or Secret Safety prompts;
That NATURE's *great Command* may be obey'd,
Nor all the sweet Sensations they perceive
Indulg'd in vain. Some to the Holly-Hedge
Nestling repair, and to the Thicket some;
Some to the rude Protection of the Thorn
Commit their feeble Offspring. The cleft Tree
Offers its kind Concealment to a Few,
Their Food its Insects, and its Moss their Nests.
Others apart far in the grassy Dale,
Or roughening Waste, their humble Texture weave.
But most in woodland Solitudes delight,
In unfrequented Glooms, or shaggy Banks,
Steep, and divided by a babbling Brook,
Whose Murmurs soothe them all the live-long Day,
When by kind Duty fix'd. Among the Roots
Of Hazel, pendant o'er the plaintive Stream,
They frame the first Foundation of their Domes;
Dry Sprigs of Trees, in artful Fabrick laid,
And bound with Clay together. Now 'tis nought

But restless Hurry thro' the busy Air,
Beat by unumber'd Wings. The Swallow sweeps
The slimy Pool, to build his hanging House
Intent. And often, from the careless Back
Of Herds and Flocks, a thousand tugging Bills
Pluck Hair and Wool; and oft, when unobserv'd,
Steal from the Barn a Straw: till soft and warm,
Clean, and compleat, their Habitation grows.

   As thus the patient Dam assiduous sits,
Not to be tempted from her tender Task,
Or by sharp Hunger, or by smooth Delight,
Tho' the whole loosen'd Spring around Her blows,
Her sympathizing Lover takes his Stand
High on th' opponent Bank, and ceaseless sings
The tedious Time away; or else supplies
Her Place a Moment, while she sudden flits
To pick the scanty Meal. Th' appointed Time
With pious Toil fulfill'd, the callow Young,
Warm'd and expanded into perfect Life,
Their brittle Bondage break, and come to Light,
A helpless Family, demanding Food
With constant Clamour. O what Passions then,
What melting Sentiments of kindly Care,
On the new Parents seize! Away they fly
Affectionate, and undesiring bear
The most delicious Morsel to their Young,
Which equally distributed, again
The search begins.
. . . .

   But now the feather'd Youth their former Bounds,
Ardent, disdain; and, weighing oft their Wings.
Demand the free Possession of the Sky.
This one glad Office more, and then dissolves
Parental Love at once, now needless grown.
Unlavish *Wisdom* never works in vain.
'Tis on some Evening, sunny, grateful, mild,
When nought but Balm is breathing thro' the Woods,
With yellow Lustre bright, that the new Tribes
Visit the spacious Heavens, and look abroad

[183]

On Nature's Common, far as they can see,
Or wing, their Range, and Pasture. O'er the Boughs
Dancing about, still at the giddy Verge
Their Resolution fails; their Pinions still,
In loose Libration stretch'd, to trust the Void
Trembling refuse: till down before them fly
The Parent-Guides, and chide, exhort, command,
Or push them off. The surging Air receives
The plumy Burden; and their self-taught Wings
Winnow the waving Element. On Ground
Alighted, bolder up again they lead,
Farther and farther on, the lengthening Flight;
Till vanish'd every Fear, and every Power
Rouz'd into Life and Action, light in Air
Th' acquitted Parents see their soaring Race,
And once rejoicing never know them more.

JAMES THOMSON

The Question

I dreamed that, as I wandered by the way,
  Bare Winter suddenly was changed to Spring,
And gentle odours led my steps astray,
  Mixed with a sound of waters murmuring
Along a shelving bank of turf, which lay
  Under a copse, and hardly dared to fling
Its green arms round the bosom of the stream,
But kissed it and then fled, as thou mightest in a dream.

There grew pied wind-flowers and violets,
  Daisies, those pearled Arcturi of the earth,
The constellated flower that never sets;
  Faint oxslips; tender bluebells, at whose birth
The sod scarce heaved; and that tall flower that wets —
  Like a child, half in tenderness and mirth —
Its mother's face, with Heaven's collected tears,
When the low wind, its playmate's voice, it hears.

[184]

And in the warm hedge grew lush eglantine,
   Green cowbind and the moonlight-coloured may,
And cherry-blossoms, and white cups, whose wine
   Was the bright dew, yet drained not by the day;
And wild roses, and ivy serpentine,
   With its dark buds and leaves, wandering astray;
And flowers azure, black, and streaked with gold,
Fairer than any wakened eyes behold.

And nearer to the river's trembling edge
   There grew broad flag-flowers, purple pranked with white,
And starry river buds among the sedge,
   And floating water-lilies, broad and bright,
Which lit the oak that overhung the hedge
   With moonlight beams of their own watery light;
And bulrushes, and reeds of such deep green
As soothed the dazzled eye with sober sheen.

Methought that of these visionary flowers
   I made a nosegay, bound in such a way
That the same hues, which in their natural bowers
   Were mingled or opposed, the like array
Kept these imprisoned children of the Hours
   Within my hand, — and then, elate and gay,
I hastened to the spot whence I had come,
That I might there present it! — Oh! to whom?

PERCY BYSSHE SHELLEY

[185]

The Spring

When wintry weather's al a-done
An' brooks da sparkle in the zun,
An' nâisy buildèn rooks da vlee
Wi sticks toward ther elem tree,
An' we can hear birds zing, and zee
    Upon the boughs the buds o' spring,
    Then I don't envy any king,
        A-vield wi' health an' zunsheen.

Var then the cowslip's hangèn flow'r,
A-wetted in the zunny show'r,
Da grow wi' vilets sweet o' smell,
That mâidens al da like so well;
An' drushes' aggs, wi' sky-blue shell,
    Da lie in mossy nests among
    The tharns, while thē da zing ther zong
        At evemen in the zunsheen.

An' God da miake His win' to blow
An' râin to val var high an' low,
An' tell His marnen zun to rise
Var al alik'; an' groun' an' skies
Ha' colors var the poor man's eyes;
    An' in our trials He is near
    To hear our muoan an' zee our tear,
        An' turn our clouds to zunsheen.

An' many times, when I da vind
Things goo awry, and vo'ke unkind;
To see the quiet veedèn herds,
An' hear the zingèn o' the birds,
Da still my spurrit muore than words.
    Var I da zee that 'tis our sin
    Da miake oon's soul so dark 'ithin
        When God wood gie us zunsheen.

WILLIAM BARNES

'Spring goeth all in white'

Spring goeth all in white,
Crowned with milk-white may:
In fleecy flocks of light
O'er heaven the white clouds stray:

White butterflies in the air;
White daisies prank the ground:
The cherry and hoary pear
Scatter their snow around.

ROBERT BRIDGES

[187]

Spring

Frost-locked all the winter,
Seeds, and roots, and stones of fruits,
What shall make their sap ascend
That they may put forth shoots?
Tips of tender green,
Leaf, or blade, or sheath;
Telling of the hidden life
That breaks forth underneath,
Life nursed in its grave by Death.

Blows the thaw-wind pleasantly,
Drips the soaking rain,
By fits looks down the waking sun:
Young grass springs on the plain;
Young leaves clothe early hedgerow trees;
Seeds, and roots, and stones of fruits,
Swoln with sap put forth their shoots;
Curled-headed ferns sprout in the lane;
Birds sing and pair again.

There is no time like Spring,
When life's alive in everything,
Before new nestlings sing,
Before cleft swallows speed their journey back
Along the trackless track —
God guides their wing,
He spreads their table that they nothing lack, —
Before the daisy grows a common flower,
Before the sun has power
To scorch the world up in his noontide hour.

There is no time like Spring,
Like Spring that passes by;
There is no life like Spring-life born to die, —
Piercing the sod,
Clothing the uncouth clod,

Hatched in the nest,
Fledged on the windy bough,
Strong on the wing:
There is no time like Spring that passes by,
Now newly born, and now
Hastening to die.

CHRISTINA ROSSETTI

Song

The daisy now is out upon the green;
    And in the grassy lanes
    The child of April rains,
The sweet fresh-hearted violet, is smelt and loved unseen.

Along the brooks and meads, the daffodil
    Its yellow richness spreads.
    And by the fountain-heads
Of rivers, cowslips cluster round, and over every hill.

The crocus and the primrose may have gone,
    The snowdrop may be low,
    But soon the purple glow
Of hyacinths will fill the copse, and lilies watch the dawn.

And in the sweetness of the budding year,
    The cuckoo's woodland call,
    The skylark over all,
And then at eve, the nightingale, is doubly sweet and dear.

My soul is singing with the happy birds,
    And all my human powers
    Are blooming with the flowers,
My foot is on the fields and downs, among the flocks and herds.

Deep in the forest where the foliage droops,
    I wander, fill'd with joy.
    Again as when a boy,
The sunny vistas tempt me on with dim delicious hopes.

The sunny vistas, dim with hanging shade,
    And old romantic haze: —
    Again as in past days,
The spirit of immortal Spring doth every sense pervade.

Oh! do not say that this will ever cease; —
    This joy of woods and fields,
    This youth that nature yields,
Will never speak to me in vain, tho' soundly rapt in peace.

GEORGE MEREDITH

Spring

Nothing is so beautiful as Spring —
    When weeds, in wheels, shoot long and lovely and lush;
    Thrush's eggs look little low heavens, and thrush
Through the echoing timber does so rinse and wring
The ear, it strikes like lightnings to hear him sing;
    The glassy peartree leaves and blooms, they brush
    The descending blue; that blue is all in a rush
With richness; the racing lambs too have fair their fling.

What is all this juice and all this joy?
    A strain of the earth's sweet being in the beginning
In Eden garden. — Have, get, before it cloy,
    Before it cloud, Christ, lord, and sour with sinning,
Innocent mind and Mayday in girl and boy,
    Most, O maid's child, thy choice and worthy the winning.

GERARD MANLEY HOPKINS

[190]

A Backward Spring

The trees are afraid to put forth buds,
And there is timidity in the grass;
The plots lie gray where gouged by spuds,
    And whether next week will pass
Free of sly sour winds is the fret of each bush
    Of barberry waiting to bloom.

Yet the snowdrop's face betrays no gloom,
And the primrose pants in its heedless push.
Though the myrtle asks if it's worth the fight
    This year with frost and rime
    To venture one more time
On delicate leaves and buttons of white
From the selfsame bough as at last year's prime,
And never to ruminate on or remember
What happened to it in mid-December.

THOMAS HARDY

from

In Memoriam

Now fades the last long streak of snow,
    Now burgeons every maze of quick
    About the flowering squares, and thick
By ashen roots the violets blow.

Now rings the woodland loud and long,
    The distance takes a lovelier hue,
    And drowned in yonder living blue
The lark becomes a sightless song.

Now dance the lights on lawn and lea,
   The flocks are whiter down the vale,
   And milkier every milky sail
On winding stream or distant sea;

Where now the seamew pipes, or dives
   In yonder greening gleam, and fly
   The happy birds, that change their sky
To build and brood; that live their lives

From land to land; and in my breast
   Spring wakens too; and my regret
   Becomes an April violet,
And buds and blossoms like the rest.

ALFRED, LORD TENNYSON

''Tis time, I think, by Wenlock town'

'Tis time, I think, by Wenlock town
   The golden broom should blow;
The hawthorn sprinkled up and down
   Should charge the land with snow.

Spring will not wait the loiterer's time
   Who keeps so long away;
So others wear the broom and climb
   The hedgerows heaped with may.

Oh tarnish late on Wenlock Edge,
   Gold that I never see;
Lie long, high snowdrifts in the hedge
   That will not shower on me.

A. E. HOUSMAN

[192]

Summer Wind

It is a sultry day; the sun has drunk
The dew that lay upon the morning grass;
There is no rustling in the lofty elm
That canopies my dwelling, and its shade
Scarce cools me. All is silent, save the faint
And interrupted murmur of the bee,
Settling on the sick flowers, and then again
Instantly on the wing. The plants around
Feel the too potent fervors: the tall maize
Rolls up its long green leaves; the clover droops
Its tender foliage, and declines its blooms.
But far in the fierce sunshine tower the hills,
With all their growth of woods, silent and stern,
As if the scorching heat and dazzling light
Were but an element they loved. Bright clouds,
Motionless pillars of the brazen heaven —
Their bases on the mountains — their white tops
Shining in the far ether — fire the air
With a reflected radiance, and make turn
The gazer's eye away. For me, I lie
Languidly in the shade, where the thick turf,
Yet virgin from the kisses of the sun,
Retains some freshness, and I woo the wind
That still delays his coming. Why so slow,
Gentle and voluble spirit of the air?
Oh, come and breathe upon the fainting earth
Coolness and life. Is it that in his caves
He hears me? See, on yonder woody ridge,
The pine is bending his proud top, and now
Among the nearer groves, chestnut and oak
Are tossing their green boughs about. He comes;
Lo, where the grassy meadow runs in waves!
The deep distressful silence of the scene
Breaks up with mingling of unnumbered sounds
And universal motion. He is come,
Shaking a shower of blossoms from the shrubs,
And bearing on their fragrance; and he brings

Music of birds, and rustling of young boughs
And sound of swaying branches, and the voice
Of distant waterfalls. All the green herbs
Are stirring in his breath; a thousand flowers,
By the road-side and the borders of the brook,
Nod gayly to each other; glossy leaves
Are twinkling in the sun, as if the dew
Were on them yet, and silver waters break
Into small waves and sparkle as he comes.

WILLIAM CULLEN BRYANT

A Midsummer Noon
in the Australian Forest

Not a sound disturbs the air,
There is quiet everywhere;
Over plains and over woods
What a mighty stillness broods!

All the birds and insects keep
Where the coolest shadows sleep;
Even the busy ants are found
Resting in their pebbled mound;
Even the locust clingeth now
Silent to the barky bough:
Over hills and over plains
Quiet, vast and slumbrous, reigns.

Only there's a drowsy humming
From yon warm lagoon slow coming:
'Tis the dragon-hornet — see!
All bedaubed resplendently,
Yellow on a tawny ground —
Each rich spot nor square nor round,
Rudely heart-shaped, as it were
The blurred and hasty impress there

Of a vermeil-crusted seal
Dusted o'er with golden meal.
Only there's a droning where
Yon bright beetle shines in air,
Tracks it in its gleaming flight
With a slanting beam of light,
Rising in the sunshine higher,
Till its shards flame out like fire.

Every other thing is still,
Save the ever-wakeful rill,
Whose cool murmur only throws
Cooler comfort round repose;
Or some ripple in the sea
Of leafy boughs, where, lazily,
Tired summer, in her bower
Turning with the noontide hour,
Heaves a slumbrous breath ere she
Once more slumbers peacefully.

O 'tis easeful here to lie
Hidden from noon's scorching eye,
In this grassy cool recess
Musing thus of quietness.

CHARLES HARPUR

Summer Rain

Thick lay the dust, uncomfortably white,
In glaring mimicry of Arab sands.
The woods and mountains slept in hazy light;
The meadows look'd athirst and tawny tann'd;
The little rills had left their channels bare,
With scarce a pool to witness what they were;
And the shrunk river gleam'd 'mid oozy stones,
That stared like any famish'd giant's bones.

Sudden the hills grew black, and hot as stove
The air beneath; it was a toil to be.
There was a growling as of angry Jove,
Provoked by Juno's prying jealousy —
A flash — a crash — the firmament was split,
And down it came in drops — the smallest fit
To drown a bee in fox-glove bell concealed;
Joy fill'd the brook, and comfort cheer'd the field.

HARTLEY COLERIDGE

Summer

Winter is cold-hearted,
  Spring is yea and nay,
Autumn is a weather-cock
Blown every way:
Summer days for me
When every leaf is on its tree;

When Robin's not a beggar,
  And Jenny Wren's a bride,
And larks hang singing, singing, singing,
  Over the wheat-fields wide,
  And anchored lilies ride,
And the pendulum spider
  Swings from side to side,

And blue-black beetles transact business,
  And gnats fly in a host,
And furry caterpillars hasten
  That no time be lost,
And moths grow fat and thrive,
And ladybirds arrive.

SEASONS

Before green apples blush,
  Before green nuts embrown,
Why, one day in the country
  Is worth a month in town;
  Is worth a day and a year
Of the dusty, musty, lag-last fashion
  That days drone elsewhere.

CHRISTINA ROSSETTI

Heat

From plains that reel to southward, dim,
  The road runs by me white and bare;
Up the steep hill it seems to swim
  Beyond, and melt into the glare.
Upward half-way, or it may be
  Nearer the summit, slowly steals
A hay-cart, moving dustily
  With idly clacking wheels.

By his cart's side the wagoner
  Is slouching slowly at his ease,
Half-ridden in the windless blur
  Of white dust puffing to his knees.
This wagon on the height above,
  From sky to sky on either hand,
Is the sole thing that seems to move
  In all the heat-held land.

Beyond me in the fields the sun
  Soaks in the grass and hath his will;
I count the marguerites one by one;
  Even the buttercups are still.

On the brook yonder not a breath
    Disturbs the spider or the midge.
The water-bugs draw close beneath
    The cool gloom of the bridge.

Where the far elm-tree shadows flood
    Dark patches in the burning grass,
The cows, each with her peaceful cud,
    Lie waiting for the heat to pass.
From somewhere on the slope near by
    Into the pale depth of the noon
A wandering thrush slides leisurely
    His thin revolving tune.

In intervals of dream, I hear
    The cricket from the droughty ground;
The grasshoppers spin into mine ear
    A small innumerable sound.
I lift mine eyes sometimes to gaze;
    The burning sky-line blinds my sight;
The woods far off are blue with haze;
    The hills are drenched in light.

And yet to me not this or that
    Is always sharp or always sweet:
In the sloped shadow of my hat
    I lean at rest and drain the heat;
Nay more, I think some blessèd power
    Hath brought me wandering idly here:
In the full furnace of this hour
    My thoughts grow keen and clear.

ARCHIBALD LAMPMAN

The Rainy Summer

There's much afoot in heaven and earth this year;
  The winds hunt up the sun, hunt up the moon,
Trouble the dubious dawn, hasten the drear
  Height of a threatening noon.

No breath of boughs, no breath of leaves, of fronds
  May linger or grow warm; the trees are loud;
The forest, rooted, tosses in her bonds,
  And strains against the cloud.

No scents may pause within the garden-fold;
  The rifled flowers are cold as ocean-shells;
Bees, humming in the storm, carry their cold
  Wild honey to cold cells.

ALICE MEYNELL

from

The Seasons — Autumn

  Now, by the cool declining Year condens'd,
Descend the copious Exhalations, check'd
As up the middle Sky unseen they stole,
And roll the doubling Fogs around the Hill.
No more the Mountain, horrid, vast, sublime,
Who pours a Sweep of Rivers from his Sides,
And high between contending Kingdoms rears
The rocky long Division, fills the View
With great Variety; but in a Night
Of gathering Vapour, from the baffled Sense,
Sinks dark and dreary. Thence expanding far,
The huge Dusk, gradual, swallows up the Plain.

Vanish the Woods. The dim-seen River seems
Sullen, and slow, to rowl the misty Wave.
Even in the Height of Noon opprest, the Sun
Sheds weak, and blunt, his wide-refracted Ray;
Whence glaring oft, with many a broaden'd Orb,
He frights the Nations. Indistinct on Earth,
Seen thro' the turbid Air, beyond the Life,
Objects appear; and, wilder'd, o'er the Waste
The Shepherd stalks gigantic. Till at last
Wreath'd dun around, in deeper Circles still
Successive closing, sits the general Fog
Unbounded o'er the World; and, mingling thick,
A formless grey Confusion covers all.

JAMES THOMSON

September 1819

The sylvan slopes with corn-clad fields
Are hung, as if with golden shields,
Bright trophies of the sun!
Like a fair sister of the sky,
Unruffled doth the blue lake lie,
The mountains looking on.

And, sooth to say, yon vocal grove,
Albeit uninspired by love,
By love untaught to ring,
May well afford to mortal ear
An impulse more profoundly dear
Than music of the Spring.

For *that* from turbulence and heat
Proceeds, from some uneasy seat
In nature's struggling frame,
Some region of impatient life:
And jealousy, and quivering strife,
Therein a portion claim.

This, this is holy; — while I hear
These vespers of another year,
This hymn of thanks and praise,
My spirit seems to mount above
The anxieties of human love,
And earth's precarious days.

But list! — though winter storms be nigh,
Unchecked is that soft harmony:
There lives Who can provide
For all his creatures; and in Him,
Even like the radiant Seraphim,
These choristers confide.

WILLIAM WORDSWORTH

To Autumn

Season of mists and mellow fruitfulness!
  Close bosom-friend of the maturing sun;
Conspiring with him how to load and bless
  With fruit the vines that round the thatch-eaves run;
To bend with apples the moss'd cottage-trees,
  And fill all fruit with ripeness to the core;
    To swell the gourd, and plump the hazel shells
  With a sweet kernel; to set budding more,
And still more, later flowers for the bees,
Until they think warm days will never cease,
    For Summer has o'er-brimm'd their clammy cells.

Who hath not seen thee oft amid thy store?
  Sometimes whoever seeks abroad may find
Thee sitting careless on a granary floor,
  Thy hair soft-lifted by the winnowing wind;
Or on a half-reap'd furrow sound asleep,
  Drowsed with the fume of poppies, while thy hook
    Spares the next swath and all its twined flowers;

And sometime like a gleaner thou dost keep
  Steady thy laden head across a brook;
  Or by a cider-press, with patient look,
    Thou watchest the last oozings, hours by hours.

Where are the songs of Spring? Ay, where are they?
  Think not of them, thou hast thy music too,
While barred clouds bloom the soft-dying day,
  And touch the stubble-plains with rosy hue;
Then in a wailful choir the small gnats mourn
  Among the river sallows, borne aloft
    Or sinking as the light wind lives or dies;
And full-grown lambs loud bleat from hilly bourn;
  Hedge-crickets sing; and now with treble soft
  The redbreast whistles from a garden-croft,
    And gathering swallows twitter in the skies.

JOHN KEATS

Autumn

Siren of sullen moods and fading hues,
Yet haply not incapable of joy,
    Sweet Autumn! I thee hail
    With welcome all unfeigned;

And oft as morning from her lattice peeps
To beckon up the sun, I seek with thee
    To drink the dewy breath
    Of fields left fragrant then,

In solitudes, where no frequented paths
But what thy own foot makes betray thy home,
    Stealing obtrusive there
    To meditate thy end:

By overshadowed ponds, in woody nooks,
With ramping sallows lined, and crowding sedge,
    Which woo the winds to play,
    And with them dance for joy;

And meadow pools, torn wide by lawless floods,
Where water-lilies spread their oily leaves,
    On which, as wont, the fly
    Oft battens in the sun;

Where leans the mossy willow half-way o'er,
On which the shepherd crawls astride to throw
    His angle clear of weeds
    That crowd the water's brim;

Or crispy hills, and hollows scant of sward,
Where step by step the patient lonely boy
    Hath cut rude flights of stairs
    To climb their steepy sides;

Then track along their feet, grown hoarse with noise,
The crawling brook, that ekes its weary speed,
    And struggles through the weeds
    With faint and sullen brawl.

[203]

These haunts I long have favoured, more as now
With thee thus wandering, moralizing on,
    Stealing glad thoughts from grief,
    And happy, though I sigh.

Sweet Vision, with the wild dishevelled hair,
And raiment shadowy of each wind's embrace,
    Fain would I win thine harp
    To one accordant theme;

Now not inaptly craved, communing thus
Beneath the curdled arms of this stunt oak,
    While pillowed on the grass,
    We fondly ruminate

O'er the disordered scenes of woods and fields,
Ploughed lands, thin travelled with half-hungry sheep,
    Pastures tracked deep with cows,
    Where small birds seek for seed:

Marking the cow-boy that so merry trills
His frequent, unpremeditated song,
    Wooing the winds to pause,
    Till echo brawls again;

As on with plashy step and clouted shoon
He roves, half indolent and self-employed,
    To rob the little birds
    Of hips and pendant haws,

And sloes, dim covered as with dewy veils,
And rambling bramble-berries, pulp and sweet,
    Arching their prickly trails
    Half o'er the narrow lane:

Noting the hedger front with stubborn face
The dank blea wind, that whistles thinly by
    His leathern garb, thorn-proof,
    And cheek red-hot with toil.

While o'er the pleachy lands of mellow brown,
The mower's stubbling scythe clogs to his foot
    The ever eking wisp,
    With sharp and sudden jerk,

Till into formal rows the russet shocks
Crowd the blank field to thatch time-weathered barns,
    And hovels rude repair,
    Stript by disturbing winds.

See! from the rustling scythe the haunted hare
Scampers circuitous, with startled ears
    Prickt up, then squat, as by
    She brushes to the woods,

Where reeded grass, breast-high and undisturbed,
Forms pleasant clumps, through which the soothing winds
    Soften her rigid fears,
    And lull to calm repose.

Wild sorceress! me thy restless mood delights
More than the stir of summer's crowded scenes,
    Where, jostled in the din,
    Joy palled my ear with song;

Heart-sickening for the silence that is thine,
Not broken inharmoniously, as now
    That lone and vagrant bee
    Booms faint with weary chime.

Now filtering winds thin winnow through the woods
In tremulous noise, that bids, at every breath,
    Some sickly cankered leaf
    Let go its hold, and die.

And now the bickering storm, with sudden start,
In flirting fits of anger carps aloud,
    Thee urging to thine end,
    Sore wept by troubled skies.

[205]

And yet, sublime in grief, thy thoughts delight
To show me visions of most gorgeous dyes,
    Haply forgetting now
    They but prepare thy shroud;

Thy pencil dashing its excess of shades,
Improvident of waste, till every bough
    Burns with thy mellow touch
    Disorderly divine.

Soon must I view thee as a pleasant dream
Droop faintly, and so sicken for thine end,
    As sad the winds sink low
    In dirges for their queen;

While in the moment of their weary pause,
To cheer thy bankrupt pomp, the willing lark
    Starts from his shielding clod,
    Snatching sweet scraps of song.

Thy life is waning now, and silence tries
To mourn, but meets no sympathy in sounds,
    As stooping low she bends,
    Forming with leaves thy grave;

To sleep inglorious there mid tangled woods,
Till parch-lipped summer pines in drought away,
    Then from thine ivied trance
    Awake to glories new.

JOHN CLARE

Autumn

I saw old Autumn in the misty morn
Stand shadowless like Silence, listening
To silence, for no lonely bird would sing
Into his hollow ear from woods forlorn,
Nor lowly hedge nor solitary thorn; —
Shaking his languid locks all dewy bright
With tangled gossamer that fell by night,
    Pearling his coronet of golden corn.

Where are the songs of Summer? — With the sun,
Oping the dusky eyelids of the South,
Till shade and silence waken up as one,
And Morning sings with a warm odorous mouth.
Where are the merry birds? — Away, away,
On panting wings through the inclement skies,
    Lest owls should prey
    Undazzled at noonday,
And tear with horny beak their lustrous eyes.

Where are the blooms of Summer? — In the West,
Blushing their last to the last sunny hours,
When the mild Eve by sudden Night is prest
Like tearful Proserpine, snatch'd from her flow'rs
    To a most gloomy breast.
Where is the pride of Summer, — the green prime, —
The many, many leaves all twinkling? — Three
On the moss'd elm; three on the naked lime
Trembling, — and one upon the old oak-tree!
    Where is the Dryad's immortality? —
Gone into mournful cypress and dark yew,
Or wearing the long gloomy Winter through
    In the smooth holly's green eternity.

The squirrel gloats on his accomplish'd hoard,
The ants have brimm'd their garners with ripe grain,
    And honey bees have stored
     The sweets of Summer in their luscious cells;
     The swallows all have wing'd across the main;
    But here the autumn Melancholy dwells,
       And sighs her tearful spells,
Amongst the sunless shadows of the plain.

    Alone, alone,
     Upon a mossy stone,
She sits and reckons up the dead and gone
With the last leaves for a love-rosary,
Whilst all the wither'd world looks drearily,
Like a dim picture of the drownèd past
In the hush'd mind's mysterious far away,
Doubtful what ghostly thing will steal the last
Into that distance, gray upon the gray.

O go and sit with her, and be o'ershaded
Under the languid downfall of her hair!
She wears a coronal of flowers faded
Upon her forehead, and a face of care: —
There is enough of wither'd everywhere
To make her bower, — and enough of gloom;
There is enough of sadness to invite,
If only for the rose that died, whose doom
Is Beauty's, — she that with the living bloom
Of conscious cheeks most beautifies the light:
There is enough of sorrowing, and quite
Enough of bitter fruits the earth doth bear, —
Enough of chilly droppings for her bowl;
Enough of fear and shadowy despair,
To frame her cloudy prison for the soul!

                    THOMAS HOOD

A Threnody
Celebrating the Fall of the Leaf

No longer the nightingales chant
  To the silvery pulses of night,
That echo the measure and grant
  Responsal of starry delight:
No nightingales longer descant
  To the stars as they throb with delight
Of the passionate answer they grant
  The music that troubles the night —
As they vibrate and bloom with delight
  In the hanging gardens of night.
For the silences, harvested, throng,
  Though the gold and purpureal dye —
  Though the lacquer, the mordant, and dye
Of the autumn, like sounds of a song
  Into colour transmutable, lie
On the Forest — the crystalline tune
  That the spheres were imagined to play
Into colour transformed in the noon
  Of an ever adventurous day;
Above and within and about,
  The perfected silences throng —
In the Forest the silences throng:
No throstle, no blackbird devout
  As the seraphim mingle their song,
With perfume entangle the light
  And powder the woodland with pearl,
Nor usher the star-stricken night
With incense and melody rare;
  The song-thrush devout and the merle
No longer enrapture the air
  With concord of ruby and pearl;

Nor now can the nightingale sing
   Expecting a stellar reply;
No fugues intergarlanded ring
   Of the earth and the clusters on high —
Sidereal echoes that bring
   The crystalline tears and the sigh
For the end of a beautiful thing
   That soldered the earth and the sky.

JOHN DAVIDSON

Autumn

A touch of cold in the Autumn night —
I walked abroad,
And saw the ruddy moon lean over a hedge
Like a red-faced farmer.
I did not stop to speak, but nodded,
And round about were the wistful stars
With white faces like town children.

T. E. HULME

November

The lonely season in lonely lands, when fled
Are half the birds, and mists lie low, and the sun
Is rarely seen, nor strayeth far from his bed;
The short days pass unwelcomed one by one.

  Out by the ricks the mantled engine stands
Crestfallen, deserted, — for now all hands
Are told to the plough, — and ere it is dawn appear
The teams following and crossing far and near,
As hour by hour they broaden the brown bands

[210]

Of the striped fields; and behind them firk and prance
The heavy rooks, and daws grey-pated dance:
As awhile, surmounting a crest, in sharp outline
(A miniature of toil, a gem's design)
They are pictured, horses and men, or now near by
Above the lane they shout lifting the share,
By the trim hedgerow bloomed with purple air;
Where, under the thorns, dead leaves in huddle lie
Packed by the gales of autumn, and in and out
The small wrens glide
With a happy note of cheer,
And yellow amorets flutter above and about,
Gay, familiar in fear.

   And now, if the night shall be cold, across the sky
Linnets and twites, in small flocks helter-skelter,
All the afternoon to the gardens fly,
From thistle-pastures hurrying to gain the shelter
Of American rhododendron or cherry-laurel:
And here and there, near chilly setting of sun,
In an isolated tree a congregation
Of starlings chatter and chide,
Thickset as summer leaves, in garrulous quarrel:
Suddenly they hush as one —
The tree top springs —
And off, with a whirr of wings,
They fly by the score
To the holly-thicket, and there with myriads more
Dispute for the roosts; and from the unseen nation
A babel of tongues, like running water unceasing,
Makes live the wood, the flocking cries increasing,
Wrangling discordantly, incessantly,
While falls the night on them self-occupied;
The long dark night, that lengthens slow,
Deepening with winter to starve grass and tree,
And soon to bury in snow
The Earth, that, sleeping 'neath her frozen stole,
Shall dream a dream crept from the sunless pole
Of how her end shall be.

ROBERT BRIDGES

In November

With loitering step and quiet eye,
Beneath the low November sky,
I wandered in the woods, and found
A clearing, where the broken ground
Was scattered with black stumps and briers,
And the old wreck of forest fires.
It was a bleak and sandy spot,
And, all about, the vacant plot
Was peopled and inhabited
By scores of mulleins long since dead.
A silent and forsaken brood
In that mute opening of the wood,
So shrivelled and so thin they were,
So grey, so haggard, and austere,
Not plants at all they seemed to me,
But rather some spare company
Of hermit folk, who long ago,
Wandering in bodies to and fro,
Had chanced upon this lonely way,
And rested thus, till death one day
Surprised them at their compline prayer,
And left them standing lifeless there.

There was no sound about the wood
Save the wind's secret stir. I stood
Among the mullein-stalks as still
As if myself had grown to be
One of their sombre company,
A body without wish or will.

And as I stood, quite suddenly,
Down from a furrow in the sky
The sun shone out a little space
Across that silent sober place,
Over the sand heaps and brown sod,
The mulleins and dead goldenrod,
And passed beyond the thickets grey,
And lit the fallen leaves that lay,
Level and deep within the wood,
A rustling yellow multitude.

And all around me the thin light,
So sere, so melancholy bright,
Fell like the half-reflected gleam
Or shadow of some former dream;
A moment's golden reverie
Poured out on every plant and tree
A semblance of weird joy, or less,
A sort of spectral happiness;
And I, too, standing idly there,
With muffled hands in the chill air,
Felt the warm glow about my feet,
And shuddering betwixt cold and heat,
Drew my thoughts closer, like a cloak,
While something in my blood awoke,
A nameless and unnatural cheer,
A pleasure secret and austere.

ARCHIBALD LAMPMAN

At Day-close in November

The ten hours' light is abating,
  And a late bird wings across,
Where the pines, like waltzers waiting,
  Give their black heads a toss.

Beech leaves, that yellow the noon-time,
  Float past like specks in the eye;
I set every tree in my June time,
  And now they obscure the sky.

And the children who ramble through here
  Conceive that there never has been
A time when no tall trees grew here,
  That none will in time be seen.

THOMAS HARDY

from

The Task

The night was winter in his roughest mood;
The morning sharp and clear. But now at noon
Upon the southern side of the slant hills,
And where the woods fence off the northern blast.
The season smiles, resigning all its rage,
And has the warmth of May. The vault is blue
Without a cloud, and white without a speck
The dazzling splendour of the scene below.
Again the harmony comes o'er the vale;
And through the trees I view th' embattled tow'r
Whence all the music. I again perceive
The soothing influence of the wafted strains,
And settle in soft musings as I tread
The walk, still verdant, under oaks and elms,
Whose outspread branches overarch the glade.
The roof, though moveable through all its length
As the wind sways it, has yet well suffic'd,
And, intercepting in their silent fall
The frequent flakes, has kept a path for me.
No noise is here, or none that hinders thought.
The redbreast warbles still, but is content
With slender notes, and more than half suppress'd:
Pleas'd with his solitude, and flitting light
From spray to spray, where'er he rests he shakes
From many a twig the pendent drops of ice,
That tinkle in the wither'd leaves below.
Stillness, accompanied with sounds so soft,
Charms more than silence. Meditation here
May think down hours to moments. Here the heart
May give an useful lesson to the head,
And learning wiser grow without his books.

WILLIAM COWPER

The Snowstorm

Announced by all the trumpets of the sky,
Arrives the snow, and, driving o'er the fields,
Seems nowhere to alight: the whited air
Hides hills and woods, the river, and the heaven,
And veils the farm-house at the garden's end.
The sled and traveller stopped, the courier's feet
Delayed, all friends shut out, the housemates sit
Around the radiant fireplace, enclosed
In a tumultuous privacy of storm.

Come see the north wind's masonry.
Out of an unseen quarry evermore
Furnished with tile, the fierce artificer
Curves his white bastions with projected roof
Round every windward stake, or tree, or door.
Speeding, the myriad-handed, his wild work
So fanciful, so savage, naught cares he
For number or proportion. Mockingly,
On coop or kennel he hangs Parian wreaths;
A swan-like form invests the hidden thorn;
Fills up the farmer's lane from wall to wall,
Maugre the farmer's sighs; and, at the gate,
A tapering turret overtops the work.
And when his hours are numbered, and the world
Is all his own, retiring, as he were not,
Leaves, when the sun appears, astonished Art
To mimic in slow structures, stone by stone,
Built in an age, the mad wind's night-work,
The frolic architecture of the snow.

RALPH WALDO EMERSON

Winter Memories

Within the circuit of this plodding life
There enter moments of an azure hue,
Untarnished fair as is the violet
Or anemone, when the spring strews them
By some meandering rivulet, which make
The best philosophy untrue that aims
But to console man for his grievances.
I have remembered when the winter came,
High in my chamber in the frosty nights,
When in the still light of the cheerful moon
On every twig and rail and jutting spout,
The icy spears were adding to their length
Against the arrows of the coming sun, —
How in the shimmering noon of summer past
Some unrecorded beam slanted across
The upland pastures where the johnswort grew;
Or heard, amid the verdure of my mind,
The bee's long smothered hum, on the blue flag
Loitering amidst the mead; or busy rill,
Which now through all its course stands still and dumb,
Its own memorial, — purling at its play
Along the slopes, and through the meadows next,
Until its youthful sound was hushed at last
In the staid current of the lowland stream;
Or seen the furrows shine but late upturned,
And where the fieldfare followed in the rear,
When all the fields around lay bound and hoar
Beneath a thick integument of snow: —
So by God's cheap economy made rich,
To go upon my winter's task again.

HENRY DAVID THOREAU

Snowflakes

Out of the bosom of the Air,
  Out of the cloud-folds of her garments shaken,
Over the woodlands brown and bare,
  Over the harvest-fields forsaken,
    Silent, and soft, and slow
    Descends the snow.

Even as our cloudy fancies take
  Suddenly shape in some divine expression,
Even as the troubled heart doth make
  In the white countenance confession,
    The troubled sky reveals
    The grief it feels.

This is the poem of the Air,
  Slowly in silent syllables recorded;
This is the secret of despair,
  Long in its cloudy bosom hoarded,
    Now whispered and revealed
    To wood and field.

H. W. LONGFELLOW

How one Winter came
in the Lake Region

For weeks and weeks the autumn world stood still,
  Clothed in the shadow of a smoky haze;
The fields were dead, the wind had lost its will,
And all the lands were hushed by wood and hill,
  In those grey, withered days.

[218]

SEASONS

Behind a mist the blear sun rose and set,
  At night the moon would nestle in a cloud;
The fisherman, a ghost, did cast his net;
The lake its shores forgot to chafe and fret,
  And hushed its caverns loud.

Far in the smoky woods the birds were mute,
  Save that from blackened tree a jay would scream,
Or far in swamps the lizard's lonesome lute
Would pipe in thirst, or by some gnarled root
  The tree-toad trilled his dream.

From day to day still hushed the season's mood,
  The streams stayed in their runnels shrunk and dry;
Suns rose aghast by wave and shore and wood,
And all the world, with ominous silence, stood
  In weird expectancy.

When one strange night the sun like blood went down,
  Flooding the heavens in a ruddy hue;
Red grew the lake, the sere fields parched and brown,
Red grew the marshes where the creeks stole down,
  But never a wind-breath blew.

That night I felt the winter in my veins,
  A joyous tremor of the icy glow;
And woke to hear the North's wild vibrant strains,
While far and wide, by withered woods and plains,
  Fast fell the driving snow.

WILFRED CAMPBELL

To a Snowflake

What heart could have thought you? —
Past our devisal
(O filigree petal!)
Fashioned so purely,
Fragilely, surely,
From what Paradisal
Imagineless metal,
Too costly for cost?
Who hammered you, wrought you,
From argentine vapour? —
'God was my shaper.
Passing surmisal,
He hammered, He wrought me,
From curled silver vapour,
To lust of His mind: —
Thou could'st not have thought me!
So purely, so palely,
Tinily, surely,
Mightily, frailly,
Insculped and embossed,
With His hammer of wind,
And His graver of frost.'

FRANCIS THOMPSON

Winter

I, singularly moved
To love the lovely that are not beloved,
Of all the Seasons, most
Love Winter, and to trace
The sense of Trophonian pallor on her face.
It is not death, but plenitude of peace;
And the dim cloud that does the world enfold
Hath less the characters of dark and cold

[220]

Than warmth and light asleep,
And correspondent breathing seems to keep
With the infant harvest, breathing soft below
Its eider coverlet of snow.
Nor is in field or garden anything
But, duly looked into, contains serene
The substance of things hoped for, in the Spring,
And evidence of Summer not yet seen.
On every chance-mild day
That visits the moist shaw,
The honeysuckle, 'sdaining to be crost
In urgence of sweet life by sleet or frost,
'Voids the time's law
With still increase
Of leaflet new, and little, wandering spray;
Often, in sheltering brakes,
As one from rest disturbed in the first hour,
Primrose or violet bewildered wakes,
And deems 'tis time to flower;
Though not a whisper of her voice he hear,
The buried bulb does know
The signals of the year,
And hails far Summer with his lifted spear.
The gorse-field dark, by sudden, gold caprice,
Turns, here and there, into a Jason's fleece;
Lilies, that soon in Autumn slipped their gowns of green,
And vanished into earth,
And came again, ere Autumn died, to birth,
Stand full-arrayed, amidst the wavering shower,
And perfect for the Summer, less the flower;
In nook of pale or crevice of crude bark,
Thou canst not miss,
If close thou spy, to mark
The ghostly chrysalis,
That, if thou touch it, stirs in its dream dark;
And the flushed Robin, in the evenings hoar,
Does of Love's Day, as if he saw it, sing;
But sweeter yet than dream or song of Summer or Spring
Are Winter's sometime smiles, that seem to well
From infancy ineffable;

Her wandering, languorous gaze,
So unfamiliar, so without amaze,
On the elemental, chill adversity,
The uncomprehended rudeness; and her sigh
And solemn, gathering tear,
And look of exile from some great repose, the sphere
Of ether, moved by ether only, or
By something still more tranquil.

COVENTRY PATMORE

'There's a certain slant of light'

There's a certain slant of light,
Winter afternoons —
That oppresses, like the heft
Of cathedral tunes.

Heavenly hurt it gives us —
We can find no scar,
But internal difference,
Where the meanings are.

None may teach it — any —
'Tis the seal despair —
An imperial affliction
Sent us of the air.

When it comes, the landscape listens,
Shadows hold their breath —
When it goes, 'tis like the distance
On the look of death.

EMILY DICKINSON

The Roaring Frost

A flock of winds came winging from the North,
Strong birds with fighting pinions driving forth
    With a resounding call: —

Where will they close their wings and cease their cries —
Between what warming seas and conquering skies —
    And fold, and fall?

ALICE MEYNELL

Snow

In the gloom of whiteness,
In the great silence of snow,
A child was sighing
And bitterly saying: 'Oh,
They have killed a white bird up there on her nest,
The down is fluttering from her breast!'
And still it fell through that dusky brightness
On the child crying for the bird of the snow.

EDWARD THOMAS

Section 6
LANDSCAPE

The Pine Forest
of the Cascine near Pisa

Dearest, best and brightest,
    Come away,
To the woods and to the fields!
Dearer than this fairest day
Which, like thee to those in sorrow,
Comes to bid a sweet good-morrow
To the rough Year just awake
In its cradle in the brake.

The eldest of the Hours of Spring,
Into the Winter wandering,
Looks upon the leafless wood,
And the banks all bare and rude;
Found, it seems, this halcyon Morn
In February's bosom born,
Bending from Heaven, in azure mirth,
Kissed the cold forehead of the Earth,
And smiled upon the silent sea,
And bade the frozen streams be free;
And waked to music all the fountains,
And breathed upon the rigid mountains,
And made the wintry world appear
Like one on whom thou smilest, Dear.

Radiant Sister of the Day,
Awake! arise! and come away!
To the wild woods and the plains,
To the pools where winter rains
Image all the roof of leaves,
Where the pine its garland weaves
Sapless, gray, and ivy dun
Round stems that never kiss the sun —
To the sandhills of the sea,
Where the earliest violets be.

Now the last day of many days,
All beautiful and bright as thou
The loveliest and the last, is dead,
Rise, Memory, and write its praise!
And do thy wonted work and trace
The epitaph of glory fled;
For now the Earth has changed its face,
A frown is on the Heaven's brow.

We wandered to the Pine Forest
    That skirts the Ocean's foam,
The lightest wind was in its nest,
    The tempest in its home.

The whispering waves were half asleep,
    The clouds were gone to play,
And on the woods, and on the deep
    The smile of Heaven lay.

It seemed as if the day were one
    Sent from beyond the skies,
Which shed to earth above the sun
    A light of Paradise.

We paused amid the pines that stood,
    The giants of the waste,
Tortured by storms to shapes as rude
    With stems like serpents interlaced.

How calm it was — the silence there
    By such a chain was bound,
That even the busy woodpecker
    Made stiller by her sound

The inviolable quietness;
    The breath of peace we drew
With its soft motion made not less
    The calm that round us grew.

It seemed that from the remotest seat
  Of the white mountain's waste
To the bright flower beneath our feet,
  A magic circle traced; —

A spirit interfused around,
  A thinking, silent life;
To momentary peace it bound
  Our mortal nature's strife; —

And still, it seemed, the centre of
  The magic circle there,
Was one whose being filled with love
  The breathless atmosphere.

Were not the crocuses that grew
  Under that ilex-tree
As beautiful in scent and hue
  As ever fed the bee?

We stood beneath the pools that lie
  Under the forest bough,
And each seemed like a sky
  Gulfed in a world below;

A purple firmament of light
  Which in the dark earth lay,
More boundless than the depth of night,
  And clearer than the day —

In which the massy forests grew
  As in the upper air,
More perfect both in shape and hue
  Than any waving there.

Like one beloved the scene had lent
  To the dark water's breast
Its every leaf and lineament
  With that clear truth expressed;

There lay far glades and neighbouring lawn,
   And through the dark green crowd
The white sun twinkling like the dawn
   Under a speckled cloud.

Sweet views, which in our world above
   Can never well be seen,
Were imaged by the water's love
   Of that fair forest green.

And all was interfused beneath
   With an Elysian air,
An atmosphere without a breath,
   A silence sleeping there.

Until a wandering wind crept by,
   Like an unwelcome thought,
Which from my mind's too faithful eye
   Blots thy bright image out.

For thou art good and dear and kind,
   The forest ever green,
But less of peace in S — — 's mind,
   Than calm in waters, seen.

PERCY BYSSHE SHELLEY

from

The Prairies

These are the gardens of the Desert, these
The unshorn fields, boundless and beautiful,
For which the speech of England has no name —
The Prairies. I behold them for the first,
And my heart swells, while the dilated sight
Takes in the encircling vastness. Lo! they stretch,
In airy undulations, far away,
As if the ocean, in his gentlest swell,
Stood still, with all his rounded billows fixed,
And motionless forever. — Motionless? —
No — they are all unchained again. The clouds

[231]

Sweep over with their shadows, and, beneath,
The surface rolls and fluctuates to the eye;
Dark hollows seem to glide along and chase
The sunny ridges. Breezes of the South!
Who toss the golden and the flame-like flowers,
And pass the prairie-hawk that, poised on high,
Flaps his broad wings, yet moves not — ye have played
Among the palms of Mexico and vines
Of Texas, and have crisped the limpid brooks
That from the fountains of Sonora glide
Into the calm Pacific — have ye fanned
A nobler or a lovelier scene than this?
Man hath no power in all this glorious work:
The hand that built the firmament hath heaved
And smoothed these verdant swells, and sown their slopes
With herbage, planted them with island groves,
And hedged them round with forests. Fitting floor
For this magnificent temple of the sky —
With flowers whose glory and whose multitude
Rival the constellations! The great heavens
Seem to stoop down upon the scene in love, —
A nearer vault, and of a tenderer blue,
Than that which bends above our eastern hills.

WILLIAM CULLEN BRYANT

From the Flats

What heartache — ne'er a hill!
Inexorable, vapid, vague, and chill
The drear sand-levels drain my spirit low.
With one poor word they tell me all they know;
Whereat their stupid tongues, to tease my pain,
Do drawl it o'er again and o'er again.
They hurt my heart with griefs I cannot name:
    Always the same, the same.

Nature hath no surprise,
No ambuscade of beauty 'gainst mine eyes
From brake or lurking dell or deep defile;
No humors, frolic forms — this mile, that mile;
No rich reserves or happy-valley hopes
Beyond the bends of roads, the distant slopes.
Her fancy fails, her wild is all run tame:
    Ever the same, the same.

Oh, might I through these tears
But glimpse some hill my Georgia high uprears,
Where white the quartz and pink the pebble shine,
The hickory heavenward strives, the muscadine
Swings o'er the slope, the oak's far-falling shade
Darkens the dogwood in the bottom glade,
And down the hollow from a ferny nook
    Bright leaps a living brook!

SIDNEY LANIER

Prairie

a light word
filled with wistful spokes
of sun through the overcast at dusk
or smoke totems bent at the top
wisping away into beige emulsions

an earth word
a moist darkness turning
stones and roots
fossils and tiny lives
up to the sun

a watery word
mirage and heat lightning
steadied by pewter barns

where whole towns float in a lilting haze
and rumors of rain rise from the rapeseed lakes

a flame shaped word
a ragged mane blowing
for miles across dry grass
lighting the night like fired breath
out of the old testament

a word with air
in its belly that howls
for hours or days and dries
the memory of soft conversation
to wheatdust under the tongue

like the distance we've come
to stand here in the sky at the top of the world

GEORGE AMABILE

The Fens

Wandering by the river's edge,
I love to rustle through the sedge
And through the woods of reed to tear
Almost as high as bushes are.
Yet, turning quick with shudder chill,
As danger ever does from ill,
Fear's moment ague quakes the blood,
While plop the snake coils in the flood
And, hissing with a forked tongue,
Across the river winds along.
In coat of orange, green, and blue
Now on a willow branch I view,
Grey waving to the sunny gleam,
Kingfishers watch the ripple stream
For little fish that nimble bye
And in the gravel shallows lie.

[234]

Eddies run before the boats,
Gurgling where the fisher floats,
Who takes advantage of the gale
And hoists his handkerchief for sail
On osier twigs that form a mast —
While idly lies, nor wanted more,
The spirit that pushed him on before.

There's not a hill in all the view,
Save that a forked cloud or two
Upon the verge of distance lies
And into mountains cheats the eyes.
And as to trees the willows wear
Lopped heads as high as bushes are;
Some taller things the distance shrouds
That may be trees or stacks or clouds
Or may be nothing; still they wear
A semblance where there's nought to spare.
Among the tawny tasselled reed
The ducks and ducklings float and feed.
With head oft dabbing in the flood
They fish all day the weedy mud,
And tumbler-like are bobbing there,
Heels topsy-turvy in the air.

The geese in troops come droving up,
Nibble the weeds, and take a sup;
And, closely puzzled to agree,
Chatter like gossips over tea.
The gander with his scarlet nose
When strife's at height will interpose,
And, stretching neck to that and this,
Will now a mutter, now a hiss,
A nibble at the feathers too,
A sort of 'pray be quiet do',
And turning as the matter mends,
He stills them into mutual friends;
Then in sort of triumph sings
And throws the water o'er his wings.

[235]

LANDSCAPE

Ah, could I see a spinney nigh,
A puddock riding in the sky
Above the oaks with easy sail
On stilly wings and forked tail,
Or meet a heath of furze in flower,
I might enjoy a quiet hour,
Sit down at rest, and walk at ease,
And find a many things to please.
But here my fancy's moods admire
The naked levels till they tire,
Nor e'en a molehill cushion meet
To rest on when I want a seat.

Here's little save the river scene
And grounds of oats in rustling green
And crowded growth of wheat and beans,
That with the hope of plenty leans
And cheers the farmer's gazing brow,
Who lives and triumphs in the plough —
One sometimes meets a pleasant sward
Of swarthy grass; and quickly marred
The plough soon turns it into brown,
And, when again one rambles down
The path, small hillocks burning lie
And smoke beneath a burning sky.
Green paddocks have but little charms
With gain the merchandise of farms;
And, muse and marvel where we may,
Gain mars the landscape every day —
The meadow grass turned up and copt,
The trees to stumpy dotterels lopt,
The hearth with fuel to supply
For rest to smoke and chatter bye;
Giving the joy of home delights,
The warmest mirth on coldest nights.
And so for gain, that joy's repay,
Change cheats the landscape every day,
Nor trees nor bush about it grows
That from the hatchet can repose,

[236]

And the horizon stooping smiles
O'er treeless fens of many miles.
Spring comes and goes and comes again
And all is nakedness and fen.

JOHN CLARE

The Marshes of Glynn

Glooms of the live-oaks, beautiful-braided and woven
With intricate shades of the vines that myriad-cloven
    Clamber the forks of the multiform boughs, —
        Emerald twilights, —
        Virginal shy lights,
Wrought of the leaves to allure to the whisper of vows,
When lovers pace timidly down through the green colonnades
    Of the dim sweet woods, of the dear dark woods,
        Of the heavenly woods and glades,
    That run to the radiant marginal sand-beach within
        The wide sea-marshes of Glynn; —

    Beautiful glooms, soft dusks in the noon-day fire, —
    Wildwood privacies, closets of lone desire,
Chamber from chamber parted with wavering arras of leaves, —
Cells for the passionate pleasure of prayer to the soul that grieves,
    Pure with a sense of the passing of saints through the wood,
    Cool for the dutiful weighing of ill with good; —

O braided dusks of the oak and woven shades of the vine.
While the riotous noon-day sun of the June-day long did shine,
Ye held me fast in your heart and I held you fast in mine;
    But now when the noon is no more, and riot is rest,
    And the sun is a-wait at the ponderous gate of the West,
        And the slant yellow beam down the wood-aisle doth
        seem
        Like a lane into heaven that leads from a dream, —

Ay, now, when my soul all day hath drunken the soul of the oak,
And my heart is at ease from men, and the wearisome sound of the
       stroke
    Of the scythe of time and the trowel of trade is low,
    And belief overmasters doubt, and I know that I know,
    And my spirit is grown to a lordly great compass within,
    That the length and the breadth and the sweep of the marshes
      of Glynn
    Will work me no fear like the fear they have wrought me of
      yore
        When length was fatigue, and when breadth was but
          bitterness sore,
        And when terror and shrinking and dreary unnamable
          pain
Drew over me out of the merciless miles of the plain, —
      Oh, now, unafraid, I am fain to face
        The vast sweet visage of space.
    To the edge of the wood I am drawn, I am drawn,
    Where the gray beach glimmering runs, as a belt of the dawn,
        For a mete and a mark
        To the forest-dark: —
           So:
        Affable live-oak, leaning low, —
    Thus — with your favor — soft, with a reverent hand,
    (Not lightly touching your person, Lord of the land!)
    Bending your beauty aside, with a step I stand
        On the firm-packed sand,
          Free
        By a world of marsh that borders a world of sea.
    Sinuous southward and sinuous northward the shimmering
      band
    Of the sand-beach fastens the fringe of the marsh to the folds
      of the land.

Inward and outward to northward and southward the beach-lines
       linger and curl
As a silver-wrought garment that clings to and follows the firm
       sweet limbs of a girl.
Vanishing, swerving, evermore curving again into sight,
Softly the sand-beach wavers away to a dim gray looping of light.

And what if behind me to westward the wall of the woods stands
       high?
The world lies east: how ample, the marsh and the sea and the sky!
    A league and a league of marsh-grass, waist-high, broad in the
        blade,
    Green, and all of a height, and unflecked with a light or a
        shade,
        Stretch leisurely off, in a pleasant plain,
        To the terminal blue of the main.

      Oh, what is abroad in the marsh and the terminal sea?
        Somehow my soul seems suddenly free
    From the weighing of fate and the sad discussion of sin,
    By the length and the breadth and the sweep of the marshes of
        Glynn.
Ye marshes, how candid and simple and nothing-withholding and
        free
Ye publish yourselves to the sky and offer yourselves to the sea!
Tolerant plains, that suffer the sea and the rains and the sun,
Ye spread and span like the catholic man who hath mightily won
    God out of knowledge and good out of infinite pain
    And sight out of blindness and purity out of a stain.

    As the marsh-hen secretly builds on the watery sod,
    Behold I will build me a nest on the greatness of God:
    I will fly in the greatness of God as the marsh-hen flies
    In the freedom that fills all the space 'twixt the marsh and the
        skies:
    By so many roots as the marsh-grass sends in the sod
    I will heartily lay me a-hold on the greatness of God:
    Oh, like to the greatness of God is the greatness within
    The range of the marshes, the liberal marshes of Glynn.

And the sea lends large, as the marsh: lo, out of his plenty the sea
    Pours fast: full soon the time of the flood-tide must be:
        Look how the grace of the sea doth go
    About and about through the intricate channels that flow
        Here and there,
        Everywhere,

Till his waters have flooded the uttermost creeks and the low-lying
   lanes,
  And the marsh is meshed with a million veins,
 That like as with rosy and silvery essences flow
  In the rose-and-silver evening glow.
    Farewell, my lord Sun!
 The creeks overflow: a thousand rivulets run
 'Twixt the roots of the sod; the blades of the marsh-grass stir;
Passeth a hurrying sound of wings that westward whirr;
Passeth, and all is still; and the currents cease to run;
  And the sea and the marsh are one.
  How still the plains of the waters be!
  The tide is in his ecstasy.
  The tide is at his highest height:
   And it is night.

  And now from the Vast of the Lord will the waters of sleep
   Roll in on the souls of men,
  But who will reveal to our waking ken
  The forms that swim and the shapes that creep
   Under the waters of sleep?
And I would I could know what swimmeth below when the tide
   comes in
  On the length and the breadth of the marvellous marshes of
   Glynn.

SIDNEY LANIER

The Winter Shore

A mighty change it is, and ominous
Of mightier, sleeping in Eternity.
The bare cliffs seem half-sinking in the sand,
Heaved high by winter seas; and their white crowns,
Struck by the whirlwinds, shed their hair-like snow
Upon the desolate air. Sullen and black,
Their huge backs rearing far along the waves,
The rocks lie barrenly, which there have lain,
Revealed, or hidden, from immemorial time;
And o'er them hangs a sea-weed drapery,
Like some old Triton's hair, beneath which lurk
Myriads of crownèd shell-fish, things whose life,
Like a celled hermit's, seemeth profitless.
Vast slimy masses hardened into stone
Rise smoothly from the surface of the Deep,
Each with a hundred thousand fairy cells
Perforate, like a honeycomb, and, cup-like,
Filled with the sea's salt crystal — the soft beds
Once of so many pebbles, thence divorced
By the continual waters, as they grew
Slowly to rock. The bleak shore is o'erspread
With sea-weeds green and sere, curled and dishevelled,
As they were mermaids' tresses, wildly torn
For some sea-sorrow. The small mountain-stream,
Swoln to a river, laves the quivering beach,
And flows in many channels to the sea
Between high shingly banks, that shake for ever.
The solitary sea-bird, like a spirit,
Balanced in air upon his crescent wings,
Hangs floating in the winds, as he were lord
Of the drear vastness round him, and alone
Natured for such dominion. Spring and Summer
And storèd Autumn, of their liveries
Here is no vestige; Winter, tempest-robed,
In gloomy grandeur o'er the hills and seas
Reigneth omnipotent.

THOMAS WADE

[241]

The Quiet Tide near Ardrossan

On to the beach the quiet waters crept:
But, though I stood not far within the land,
No tidal murmur reach'd me from the strand.
The mirror'd clouds beneath old Arran slept.
I look'd again across the watery waste:
The shores were full, the tide was near its height,
Though scarcely heard: the reefs were drowning fast,
And an imperial whisper told the might
Of the outer floods, that press'd into the bay,
Though all besides was silent. I delight
In the rough billows, and the foam-ball's flight:
I love the shore upon a stormy day;
But yet more stately were the power and ease
That with a whisper deepen'd all the seas.

CHARLES TENNYSON TURNER

A Walk
on the Machair of North Uist

Stereophonic skylark music,
sea pinks and silverweed
vast carpets of daisies,
the tractor with its trailer
piled high with seaweed.
Squeaky lapwings, strident redshanks,
bubbling curlews, jangling corn buntings,
I almost tread on
an oystercatcher's eggs.
Tiny footprints in the sand
mingling with my own
as ringed plovers scurry
back and forth.
A corncrake grates —
no chance of seeing him
among the irises.
A rabbit scuttles away.
Gulls aplenty, stiff-winged fulmars,
turnstone, dunlin, rock pipit,
shelduck, eider, shag,
cormorant, hoodie, wheatear;
I search in vain for red-necked phalaropes.
An arctic tern attacks me
screeching, swooping at my head;
I sympathise — I see a
solitary egg and she has come
ten thousand miles to lay it.
A disturbance in the sea
and two basking sharks appear
a stone's throw from the shore;
and because it is dull and cloudy
I have no camera.
Rocks and driftwood far inland
evidence of the fury
of the winter gales.

The vast expanse of shell-sand beach
deserted, faintly beige-coloured
in the overcast light;
and the Atlantic gently laps
against the rocks.

OWEN HARDY

from

The Wonders of the Peake

Durst I expostulate with *Providence*,
I then should ask, wherein the innocence
Of my poor undesigning infancy,
Could *Heaven* offend to such a black degree,
As for th'offence to damn me to a place
Where *Nature* only suffers in disgrace.
A *Country* so deform'd, the *Traveller*
Would swear those parts Natures *pudenda* were:
Like *Warts* and *Wens*, hills on the one side swell,
To all but *Natives* inaccessible;
Th'other a blue scrofulous scum defiles,
Flowing from th'earths impostumated boyles;
That seems the steps (Mountains on Mountains thrown)
By which the *Giants* storm'd the *Thunderers* throne,
This from that prospect seems the sulph'rous flood,
Where sinful *Sodom* and *Gomorrah* stood.

CHARLES COTTON

Helm Crag

Go up among the mountains, when the storm
Of midnight howls, but go in that wild mood,
When the soul loves tumultuous solitude,
And through the haunted air, each giant form
Of swinging pine, black rock, or ghostly cloud,
That veils some fearful cataract tumbling loud,
Seems to thy breathless heart with life imbued.
'Mid those gaunt, shapeless things thou art alone!
The mind exists, trembles through the ear,
The memory of the human world is gone
And time and space seem living only *here*.

CHRISTOPHER NORTH

Speak of the North

Speak of the North! A lonely moor
Silent and dark and trackless swells,
The waves of some wild streamlet pour
Hurriedly through its ferny dells.

Profoundly still the twilight air,
Lifeless the landscape; so we deem
Till like a phantom gliding near
A stag bends down to drink the stream.

And far away a mountain zone,
A cold, white waste of snow-drifts lies,
And one star, large and soft and lone,
Silently lights the unclouded skies.

CHARLOTTE BRONTË

[245]

The Lough

Among those mountain-skirts a league away
Lough Braccan spread, with many a silver bay
And islet green; a dark cliff, tall and bold,
Half-muffled in its cloak of ivy old,
Bastion'd the southern brink, beside a glen
Where birch and hazel hid the badger's den,
And through the moist ferns and firm hollies play'd
A rapid rivulet from light to shade.
Above the glen, and wood, and cliff, was seen,
Majestically simple and serene,
Like some great soul above the various crowd,
A purple mountain-top, at times in cloud
Or mist, as in celestial veils of thought,
Abstracted heavenward.
                              Creeps a little boat,
Along the path of evening's golden smile,
To where the shatter'd castle on its isle
May seem a broad-wing'd ship; two massive tow'rs
Lifted against the yellow light that pours
On half the lough and sloping fields, — half-laid,
Creek, bush, and crag, within the mountain shade.
Dark bramble-leaves now show a curling fringe,
And sallies wear the first autumnal tinge;
With speckled plumes high wave the crowded reeds,
Amongst whose watery stems the mallard feeds.

WILLIAM ALLINGHAM

The Winter Lakes

Out in a world of death, far to the northward lying,
  Under the sun and the moon, under the dusk and the day;
Under the glimmer of stars and the purple of sunsets dying,
  Wan and waste and white, stretch the great lakes away.

Never a bud of spring, never a laugh of summer,
  Never a dream of love, never a song of bird;
But only the silence and white, the shores that grow chiller and
    dumber,
  Wherever the ice-winds sob, and the griefs of winter are heard.

Crags that are black and wet out of the grey lake looming,
  Under the sunset's flush, and the pallid, faint glimmer of dawn;
Shadowy, ghost-like shores, where midnight surfs are booming
  Thunders of wintry woe over the spaces wan.

Lands that loom like spectres, whited regions of winter,
  Wastes of desolate woods, deserts of water and shore;
A world of winter and death, within these regions who enter,
  Lost to summer and life, go to return no more.

Moons that glimmer above, waters that lie white under,
  Miles and miles of lake far out under the night;
Foaming crests of waves, surfs that shoreward thunder,
  Shadowy shapes that flee, haunting the spaces white.

Lonely hidden bays, moon-lit, ice-rimmed, winding,
  Fringed by forests and crags, haunted by shadowy shores;
Hushed from the outward strife, where the mighty surf is grinding
  Death and hate on the rocks, as sandward and landward it
    roars.

WILFRED CAMPBELL

The Downs

O bold majestic downs, smooth, fair and lonely;
O still solitude, only matched in the skies:
   Perilous in steep places,
   Soft in the level races,
Where sweeping in phantom silence the cloudland flies;
With lovely undulation of fall and rise;
   Entrenched with thickets thorned,
By delicate miniature dainty flowers adorned!

I climb your crown, and lo! a sight surprising
Of sea in front uprising, steep and wide:
   And scattered ships ascending
   To heaven lost in the blending
Of distant blues, where water and sky divide,
Urging their engines against wind and tide,
   And all so small and slow
They seem to be wearily pointing the way they would go.

The accumulated murmur of soft plashing,
Of waves on rocks dashing and searching the sands,
   Takes my ear, in the veering
   Baffled wind, as rearing

Upright at the cliff, to the gullies and rifts he stands;
And his conquering surges scour out over the lands;
   While again at the foot of the downs
He masses his strength to recover the topmost crowns.

ROBERT BRIDGES

The Combe

The Combe was ever dark, ancient and dark.
Its mouth is stopped with bramble, thorn, and briar;
And no one scrambles over the sliding chalk
By beech and yew and perishing juniper
Down the half precipices of its sides, with roots
And rabbit holes for steps. The sun of Winter,
The moon of Summer, and all the singing birds
Except the missel-thrush that loves juniper,
Are quite shut out. But far more ancient and dark
The Combe looks since they killed the badger there,
Dug him out and gave him to the hounds,
That most ancient Briton of English beasts.

EDWARD THOMAS

Section 7
WATER
AND ITS INHABITANTS

The Waterfall

With what deep murmurs through time's silent stealth
Doth thy transparent, cool, and watery wealth
      Here flowing fall,
      And chide and call,
As if his liquid loose retinue stayed
Lingering, and were of this steep place afraid,
      The common pass
      Where, clear as glass,
      All must descend
      Not to an end;
But quickened by this deep and rocky grave,
Rise to a longer course more bright and brave.

    Dear stream! dear bank, where often I
    Have sat, and pleased my pensive eye,
    Why, since each drop of thy quick store,
    Runs thither, whence it flowed before,
    Should poor souls fear a shade or night,
    Who came, sure, from a sea of light?
    Or since those drops are all sent back
    So sure to thee, that none doth lack,
    Why should frail flesh doubt any more
    That what God takes, he'll not restore?
    O useful Element and clear!
    My sacred wash and cleanser here,
    My first consigner unto those
    Fountains of life, where the Lamb goes,
    What sublime truths, and wholesome themes
    Lodge in thy mystical, deep streams!
    Such as dull man can never find,
    Unless that Spirit lead his mind,
    Which first upon thy face did move,
    And hatched all with his quickening love.
    As this loud brook's incessant fall
    In streaming rings restagnates all,
    Which reach by course the bank, and then
    Are no more seen, just so pass men.

[253]

O my invisible estate,
My glorious liberty, still late!
Thou art the channel my soul seeks,
Not this with cataracts and creeks.

HENRY VAUGHAN

Written with a Pencil
Standing by the Fall of Fyers
near Loch Ness

Among the heathy hills and ragged woods
The roaring Fyers pours his mossy floods;
Till full he dashes on the rocky mounds,
Where, thro' a shapeless breach, his stream resounds.
As high in air the bursting torrents flow,
As deep recoiling surges foam below,
Prone down the rock the whitening sheet descends,
And viewless Echo's ear, astonished, rends.
Dim-seen, thro' rising mists and ceaseless show'rs,
The hoary cavern, wide-surrounding, lours.
Still thro' the gap the struggling river toils,
And still, below, the horrid cauldron boils —

ROBERT BURNS

The Cataract of Lodore

'How does the Water
Come down at Lodore?'
My little boy ask'd me
Thus, once on a time;
And moreover he task'd me
To tell him in rhyme.
Anon at the word,

There first came one daughter
  And then came another,
    To second and third
The request of their brother,
  And to hear how the water
    Comes down at Lodore,
    With its rush and its roar,
      As many a time
    They had seen it before.
So I told them in rhyme,
For of rhymes I had store:
  And 'twas in my vocation
    For their recreation
  That so I should sing;
  Because I was Laureate
      To them and their King.

    From its sources which well
      In the Tarn on the fell;
        From its fountains
        In the mountains,
      Its rills and its gills;
  Through moss and through brake,
      It runs and it creeps
      For a while, till it sleeps
      In its own little Lake.
  And thence at departing,
    Awakening and starting,
  It runs through the reeds
    And away it proceeds,
  Through meadow and glade,
    In sun and in shade,
And through the wood-shelter,
  Among crags in its flurry,
      Helter-skelter,
      Hurry-scurry.
  Here it comes sparkling,
  And there it comes darkling —
  Now smoking and frothing
  Its tumult and wrath in,

[255]

Till in this rapid race
On which it is bent,
It reaches the place
Of its steep descent.

The Cataract strong
Then plunges along,
Striking and raging
As if a war waging
Its caverns and rocks among:
Rising and leaping,
Sinking and creeping,
Swelling and sweeping,
Showering and springing,
Flying and flinging,
Writhing and ringing,
Eddying and whisking,
Spouting and frisking,
Turning and twisting,
    Around and around
With endless rebound!
Smiting and fighting,
A sight to delight in;
Confounding, astounding,
Dizzying and deafening the ear with its sound.

Collecting, projecting,
Receding and speeding,
And shocking and rocking,
And darting and parting,
And threading and spreading,
And whizzing and hissing,
And dripping and skipping,
And hitting and splitting,
And shining and twining,
And rattling and battling,
And shaking and quaking,
And pouring and roaring,
And waving and raving,
And tossing and crossing,

And flowing and going,
And running and stunning,
And foaming and roaming,
And dinning and spinning,
And dropping and hopping,
And working and jerking,
And guggling and struggling,
And heaving and cleaving,
And moaning and groaning;

And glittering and frittering,
And gathering and feathering,
And whitening and brightening,
And quivering and shivering,
And hurrying and skurrying,
And thundering and floundering;

Dividing and gliding and sliding,
And falling and brawling and sprawling,
And driving and riving and striving,
And sprinkling and twinkling and wrinkling,
And sounding and bounding and rounding,
And bubbling and troubling and doubling,
And grumbling and rumbling and tumbling,
And clattering and battering and shattering;

Retreating and beating and meeting and sheeting,
Delaying and straying and playing and spraying,
Advancing and prancing and glancing and dancing,
Recoiling, turmoiling and toiling and boiling,
And gleaming and streaming and steaming and beaming,
And rushing and flushing and brushing and gushing,
And flapping and rapping and clapping and slapping,
And curling and whirling and purling and twirling,
And thumping and plumping and bumping and jumping,
And dashing and flashing and splashing and clashing;
And so never ending, but always descending,
Sounds and motions for ever and ever are blending,
All at once and all o'er, with a mighty uproar,
And this way the Water comes down at Lodore.

ROBERT SOUTHEY

To the River Derwent

Among the mountains were we nursed, loved Stream
Thou near the eagle's nest — within brief sail,
I, of his bold wing floating on the gale,
Where thy deep voice could lull me! Faint the beam
Of human life when first allowed to gleam
On mortal notice. — Glory of the vale,
Such thy meek outset, with a crown, though frail,
Kept in perpetual verdure by the steam
Of thy soft breath! — Less vivid wreath entwined
Nemæan victor's brow; less bright was worn,
Meed of some Roman chief — in triumph borne
With captives chained; and shedding from his car
The sunset splendours of a finished war
Upon the proud enslavers of mankind!

WILLIAM WORDSWORTH

Green River

When breezes are soft and skies are fair,
I steal an hour from study and care,
And hie me away to the woodland scene,
Where wanders the stream with waters of green,
As if the bright fringe of herbs on its brink
Had given their stain to the waves they drink;
And they, whose meadows it murmurs through,
Have named the stream from its own fair hue.

Yet pure its waters — its shallows are bright
With colored pebbles and sparkles of light,
And clear the depths where its eddies play,
And dimples deepen and whirl away,
And the plane-tree's speckled arms o'ershoot
The swifter current that mines its root,

Through whose shifting leaves, as you walk the hill,
The quivering glimmer of sun and rill
With a sudden flash on the eye is thrown,
Like the ray that streams from the diamond-stone.
Oh, loveliest there the spring days come,
With blossoms, and birds, and wild-bees' hum;
The flowers of summer are fairest there,
And freshest the breath of the summer air;
And sweetest the golden autumn day
In silence and sunshine glides away.

Yet, fair as thou art, thou shunnest to glide,
Beautiful stream! by the village side;
But windest away from haunts of men,
To quiet valley and shaded glen;
And forest, and meadow, and slope of hill,
Around thee, are lonely, lovely, and still,
Lonely — save when, by thy rippling tides,
From thicket to thicket the angler glides;
Or the simpler comes, with basket and book,
For herbs of power on thy banks to look;
Or haply, some idle dreamer, like me,
To wander, and muse, and gaze on thee,
Still — save the chirp of birds that feed
On the river cherry and seedy reed,
And thy own wild music gushing out
With mellow murmur of fairy shout,
From dawn to the blush of another day,
Like traveller singing along his way.

That fairy music I never hear,
Nor gaze on those waters so green and clear,
And mark them winding away from sight,
Darkened with shade or flashing with light,
While o'er them the vine to its thicket clings,
And the zephyr stoops to freshen his wings,
But I wish that fate had left me free
To wander these quiet haunts with thee,
Till the eating cares of earth should depart,
And the peace of the scene pass into my heart;

[259]

And I envy thy stream, as it glides along,
Through its beautiful banks in a trance of song.

Though forced to drudge for the dregs of men,
And scrawl strange words with the barbarous pen,
And mingle among the jostling crowd,
Where the sons of strife are subtle and loud —
I often come to this quiet place,
To breathe the airs that ruffle thy face,
And gaze upon thee in silent dream,
For in thy lonely and lovely stream
An image of that calm life appears
That won my heart in my greener years.

WILLIAM CULLENT BRYANT

from

The Bothie of Tober-na-Vuolich

There is a stream, I name not its name, lest inquisitive tourist
Hunt it, and make it a lion, and get it at last into guide-books,
Springing far off from a loch unexplored in the folds of great
    mountains,
Falling two miles through rowan and stunted alder, enveloped
Then for four more in a forest of pine, where broad and ample
Spreads, to convey it, the glen with heathery slopes on both sides:
Broad and fair the stream, with occasional falls and narrows;
But, where the glen of its course approaches the vale of the river,
Met and blocked by a huge interposing mass of granite,
Scarce by a channel deep-cut, raging up, and raging onward,
Forces its flood through a passage so narrow a lady would step it.
There, across the great rocky wharves, a wooden bridge goes,
Carrying a path to the forest; below, three hundred yards, say,
Lower in level some twenty-five feet, through flats of shingle,
Stepping-stones and a cart-track cross in the open valley.

But in the interval here the boiling, pent-up water
Frees itself by a final descent, attaining a bason,
Ten feet wide and eighteen long, with whiteness and fury
Occupied partly, but mostly pellucid, pure, a mirror;
Beautiful there for the colour derived from green rocks under;
Beautiful, most of all, where beads of foam uprising
Mingle their clouds of white with the delicate hue of the stillness.
Cliff over cliff for its sides, with rowan and pendant birch boughs,
Here it lies, unthought of above at the bridge and pathway,
Still more enclosed from below by wood and rocky projection.
You are shut in, left alone with yourself and perfection of water,
Hid on all sides, left alone with yourself and the goddess of
    bathing.
  Here, the pride of the plunger, you stride the fall and clear it;
Here the delight of the bather, you roll in beaded sparklings,
Here into pure green depth drop down from lofty ledges.

A. H. CLOUGH

song from

The Brook

I come from haunts of coot and hern,
I make a sudden sally
And sparkle out among the fern,
To bicker down a valley.

By thirty hills I hurry down,
Or slip between the ridges,
By twenty thorps, a little town,
And half a hundred bridges.

Till last by Philip's farm I flow
To join the brimming river,
For men may come and men may go,
But I go on for ever.

[261]

I chatter over stony ways
In little sharps and trebles,
I bubble into eddying bays,
I babble on the pebbles.

With many a curve my banks I fret
By many a field and fallow,
And many a fairy-foreland set
With willow-weed and mallow.

I chatter, chatter, as I flow
To join the brimming river,
For men may come and men may go,
But I go on for ever.

I wind about, and in and out,
With here a blossom sailing,
And here and there a lusty trout,
And here and there a grayling,

And here and there a foamy flake
Upon me, as I travel
With many a silvery waterbreak
Above the golden gravel,

And draw them all along, and flow,
To join the brimming river,
For men may come and men may go,
But I go on for ever.

I steal by lawns and grassy plots,
I slide by hazel covers;
I move the sweet forget-me-nots
That grow for happy lovers.

I slip, I slide, I gloom, I glance,
Among my skimming swallows;
I make the netted sunbeam dance
Against my sandy shallows.

I murmur under moon and stars
In brambly wildernesses;
I linger by my shingly bars;
I loiter round my cresses;

And out again I curve and flow
To join the brimming river,
For men may come and men may go,
But I go on for ever.

ALFRED, LORD TENNYSON

Inversnaid

This darksome burn, horseback brown,
His rollrock highroad roaring down,
In coop and in comb the fleece of his foam
Flutes and low to the lake falls home.

A windpuff-bonnet of fáwn-fróth
Turns and twindles over the broth
Of a pool so pitchblack, féll-frówning,
It rounds and rounds Despair to drowning.

Degged with dew, dappled with dew
Are the groins of the braes that the brook treads through,
Wiry heathpacks, flitches of fern,
And the beadbonny ash that sits over the burn.

What would the world be, once bereft
Of wet and of wilderness? Let them be left,
O let them be left, wildness and wet;
Long live the weeds and the wilderness yet.

GERARD MANLEY HOPKINS

The Brook

Seated once by a brook, watching a child
Chiefly that paddled, I was thus beguiled.
Mellow the blackbird sang and sharp the thrush
Not far off in the oak and hazel brush,
Unseen. There was a scent like honeycomb
From mugwort dull. And down upon the dome
Of the stone the cart-horse kicks against so oft
A butterfly alighted. From aloft
He took the heat of the sun, and from below.
On the hot stone he perched contented so,
As if never a cart would pass again
That way; as if I were the last of men
And he the first of insects to have earth
And sun together and to know their worth.
I was divided between him and the gleam,
The motion, and the voices, of the stream,
The waters running frizzled over gravel,
That never vanish and for ever travel.
A grey flycatcher silent on a fence
And I sat as if we had been there since
The horseman and the horse beneath
The fir-tree-covered barrow on the heath,
The horseman and the horse with silver shoes,
Galloped the downs last. All that I could lose
I lost. And then the child's voice raised the dead.
'No one's been here before' was what she said
And what I felt, yet never should have found
A word for, while I gathered sight and sound.

EDWARD THOMAS

[264]

Hyla Brook

By June our brook's run out of song and speed
Sought for much after that, it will be found
Either to have gone groping underground
(And taken with it all the Hyla breed
That shouted in the mist a month ago,
Like ghost of sleigh-bells in a ghost of snow) —
Or flourished and come up in jewel-weed,
Weak foliage that is blown upon and bent
Even against the way its waters went.
Its bed is left a faded paper sheet
Of dead leaves stuck together by the heat —
A brook to none but who remember long.
This as it will be seen is other far
Than with brooks taken otherwhere in song.
We love the things we love for what they are.

ROBERT FROST

Wind and Wave

The wedded light and heat,
Winnowing the witless space,
Without a let,
What are they till they beat
Against the sleepy sod, and there beget
Perchance the violet!
Is the One found,
Amongst a wilderness of as happy grace,
To make Heaven's bound;
So that in Her
All which it hath of sensitively good
Is sought and understood
After the narrow modes the mighty Heavens prefer?

She, as a little breeze
Following still Night,
Ripples the spirit's cold, deep seas
Into delight;
But, in a while,
The immeasurable smile
Is broke by fresher airs to flashes blent
With darkling discontent;
And all the subtle zephyr hurries gay,
And all the heaving ocean heaves one way,
T'ward the void sky-line and an unguessed weal;
Until the vanward billows feel
The agitating shallows, and divine the goal,
And to foam roll,
And spread and stray
And traverse wildly, like delighted hands.
The fair and fleckless sands;
And so the whole
Unfathomable and immense
Triumphing tide comes at the last to reach
And burst in wind-kissed splendours on the deafening beach,
Where forms of children in first innocence
Laugh and fling pebbles on the rainbowed crest
Of its untired unrest.

COVENTRY PATMORE

from

Seaweed

When descends on the Atlantic
    The gigantic
Storm-wind of the equinox,
Landward in his wrath he scourges
    The toiling surges,
Laden with seaweed from the rocks:

From Bermuda's reefs; from edges
    Of sunken ledges,
In some far-off, bright Azore;
From Bahama, and the dashing,
    Silver-flashing
Surges of San Salvador;

From the tumbling surf, that buries
    The Orkneyan skerries,
Answering the hoarse Hebrides;
And from wrecks of ships, and drifting
    Spars, uplifting
On the desolate, rainy seas; —

Ever drifting, drifting, drifting
    On the shifting
Currents of the restless main;
Till in sheltered coves, and reaches
    Of sandy beaches,
All have found repose again.

H. W. LONGFELLOW

To a Fish of the Brooke

Why flyest thou away with fear?
Trust me there's naught of danger near,
   I have no wicked hooke
All covered with a snaring bait,
Alas, to tempt thee to thy fate,
   And dragge thee from the brooke.

O harmless tenant of the flood,
I do not wish to spill thy blood,
   For Nature unto thee
Perchance hath given a tender wife,
And children dear, to charm thy life,
   As she hath done for me.

Enjoy thy stream, O harmless fish;
And when an angler for his dish,
   Through gluttony's vile sin,
Attempts, a wretch, to pull thee OUT,
God give thee strength, O gentle trout,
   To pull the raskall IN!

JOHN WOLCOT

The Pike

From shadows of rich oaks outpeer
The moss-green bastions of the weir,
Where the quick dipper forages
In elver-peopled crevices.
And a small runlet trickling down the sluice
Gossamer music tires not to unloose.

Else round the broad pool's hush
   Nothing stirs.
Unless sometime a straggling heifer crush
Through the thronged spinny whence the pheasant whirs;
   Or martins in a flash
Come with wild mirth to dip their magical wings,
While in the shallow some doomed bulrush swings
   At whose hid root the diver vole's teeth gnash.

[269]

And nigh this toppling reed, still as the dead
  The great pike lies, the murderous patriarch,
  Watching the waterpit shelving and dark
Where through the plash his lithe bright vassals thread.

   The rose-finned roach and bluish bream
   And staring ruffe steal up the stream
   Hard by their glutted tyrant, now
   Still as a sunken bough.

    He on the sandbank lies,
     Sunning himself long hours
    With stony gorgon eyes:
     Westward the hot sun lowers.

Sudden the grey pike changes, and quivering, poises for slaughter;
  Intense terror wakens around him, the shoals scud awry, but
    there chances
  A chub unsuspecting; the prowling fins quicken, in fury he
    lances;
And the miller that opens the hatch stands amazed at the whirl in
    the water.

EDMUND BLUNDEN

from

The Fish

In a cool curving world he lies
And ripples with dark ecstasies.
The kind luxurious lapse and steal
Shapes all his universe to feel
And know and be; the clinging stream
Closes his memory, glooms his dream,
Who lips the roots o' the shore, and glides
Superb on unreturning tides.
Those silent waters weave for him
A fluctuant mutable world and dim,
Where wavering masses bulge and gape
Mysterious, and shape to shape
Dies momently through whorl and hollow,
And form and line and solid follow
Solid and line and form to dream
Fantastic down the eternal stream;
An obscure world, a shifting world,
Bulbous, or pulled to thin, or curled,
Or serpentine, or driving arrows,
Or serene slidings, or March narrows.
There slipping wave and shore are one,
And weed and mud. No ray of sun,
But glow to glow fades down the deep
(As dream to unknown dream in sleep);
Shaken translucency illumes
The hyaline of drifting glooms;
The strange soft-handed depth subdues
Drowned colour there, but black to hues,
As death to living, decomposes —
Red darkness of the heart of roses,
Blue brilliant from dead starless skies,
And gold that lies behind the eyes,
The unknown unnameable sightless white
That is the essential flame of night,

Lustreless purple, hooded green,
The myriad hues that lie between
Darkness and darkness! . . .

                              And all's one,
Gentle, embracing, quiet, dun,
The world he rests in, world he knows,
Perpetual curving. Only — grows
An eddy in that ordered falling,
A knowledge from the gloom, a calling
Weed in the wave, gleam in the mud —
The dark fire leaps along his blood;
Dateless and deathless, blind and still,
The intricate impulse works its will;
His woven world drops back; and he,
Sans providence, sans memory,
Unconscious and directly driven,
Fades to some dank sufficient heaven.

RUPERT BROOKE

Heaven

Fish (fly-replete, in depth of June,
Dawdling away their wat'ry noon)
Ponder deep wisdom, dark or clear,
Each secret fishy hope or fear.
Fish say, they have their Stream and Pond;
But is there anything Beyond?
This life cannot be All, they swear,
For how unpleasant, if it were!
One may not doubt that, somehow, Good
Shall come of Water and of Mud;
And, sure, the reverent eye must see
A Purpose in Liquidity.
We darkly know, by Faith we cry,
The future is not Wholly Dry.

[272]

Mud unto Mud! — Death eddies near —
Not here the appointed End, not here!
But somewhere, beyond Space and Time,
Is wetter water, slimier slime!
And there (they trust) there swimmeth One
Who swam ere rivers were begun,
Immense, of fishy form and mind,
Squamous, omnipotent, and kind;
And under that Almighty Fin,
The littlest fish may enter in.
Oh! never fly conceals a hook,
Fish say in the Eternal Brook,
But more than mundane weeds are there,
And mud, celestially fair;
Fat caterpillars drift around,
And Paradisal grubs are found;
Unfading moths, immortal flies,
And the worm that never dies.
And in that Heaven of all their wish,
There shall be no more land, say fish.

RUPERT BROOKE

from

Fish

Fish, oh Fish
So little matters!

Whether the waters rise and cover the earth
Or whether the waters wilt in the hollow places,
All one to you.

Aqueous, subaqueous,
Submerged
And wave-thrilled.

As the waters roll
Roll you.
The waters wash,
You wash in oneness
And never emerge.

Never know,
Never grasp.

Your life a sluice of sensation along your sides,
A flush at the flails of your fins, down the whorl of your tail,
And water wetly on fire in the grates of your gills;
Fixed water-eyes.

Even snakes lie together.

But oh, fish, that rock in water,
You lie only with the waters;
One touch.
No fingers, no hands and feet, no lips;
No tender muzzles,
No wistful bellies,
No loins of desire,
None.

You and the naked element,
Sway-wave.
Curvetting bits of tin in the evening light.

Who is it ejects his naked sperm to the naked flood?
In the wave-mother?
Who swims enwombed?
Who lies with the waters of his silent passion, womb-element?
— Fish in the waters under the earth.

What price *his* bread upon the waters?

Himself all silvery himself
In the element,
No more.

[274]

Nothing more.

Himself,
And the element.
Food, of course!
Water-eager eyes,
Mouth-gate open
And strong spine urging, driving;
And desirous belly gulping.

Fear also!
He knows fear!
Water-eyes craning,
A rush that almost screams,
Almost fish-voice
As the pike comes. . . .
Then gay fear, that turns the tail sprightly, from a shadow.

Food, and fear, and joie de vivre,
Without love.

The other way about:
Joie de vivre, and fear, and food,
All without love.

Quelle joie de vivre
Dans l'eau!
Slowly to gape through the waters,
Alone with the element;
To sink, and rise, and go to sleep with the waters;
To speak endless inaudible wavelets into the wave;
To breathe from the flood at the gills,
Fish-blood slowly running next to the flood, extracting fish-fire:
To have the element under one, like a lover;
And to spring away from a curvetting click in the air,
Provocative.
Dropping back with a slap on the face of the flood.
And merging oneself!

To be a fish!

So utterly without misgiving
To be a fish
In the waters.

Loveless, and so lively!
Born before God was love,
Or life knew loving.
Beautifully beforehand with it all.

Admitted, they swarm in companies,
Fishes.
They drive in shoals.
But soundless, and out of contact.
They exchange no word, no spasm, not even anger.
Not one touch.
Many suspended together, forever apart,
Each one alone with the waters, upon one wave with the rest.

A magnetism in the water between them only.

D. H. LAWRENCE

The Toad

With solemn hampered pace proceeding by
   The dewy garden-bed,
Like some old priest in antique finery,
   Stiff cope and jewelled head;

Thy sanctuary lamps are lit at dusk,
   Where leafy aisles are dim;
The bat's shrill piccolo, the swinging musk
   Blend with the beetle's hymn.

Aye something paramount and priestly too,
   Some cynic mystery,
Lurks in the dull skin with its dismal hue,
   The bright ascetic eye;

[276]

Thy heaving throat, thy sick repulsive glance
   Still awes thy foes around;
The eager hound starts back and looks askance,
   And whining paws the ground.

Yet thou has forfeited thy ancient ban,
   Thy mystical control;
We know thee now to be the friend of man,
   A simple homely soul;

And when we deemed thee curiously wise,
   Still chewing venomed paste,
Thou didst but crush the limbs of juicy flies
   With calm and critic taste.

A. C. BENSON

A Crocodile

Hard by the lilied Nile I saw
A duskish river dragon stretched along.
The brown habergeon of his limbs enamelled
With sanguine alamandines and rainy pearl:
And on his back there lay a young one sleeping,
No bigger than a mouse; with eyes like beads,
And a small fragment of its speckled egg
Remaining on its harmless, pulpy snout;
A thing to laugh at, as it gaped to catch
The baulking merry flies. In the iron jaws
Of the great devil-beast, like a pale soul
Fluttering in rocky hell, lightsomely flew
A snowy trochilus, with roseate beak
Tearing the hairy leeches from his throat.

THOMAS LOVELL BEDDOES

[277]

A Jellyfish

Visible, invisible,
    a fluctuating charm
an amber-tinctured amethyst
    inhabits it, your arm
approaches and it opens
    and it closes; you had meant
to catch it and it quivers;
    you abandon your intent.

MARIANNE MOORE

The Triumph of the Whale

Io! Pæan! Io! sing
To the finny people's King.
Not a mightier whale than this
In the vast Atlantic is;
Not a fatter fish than he
Flounders round the polar sea.
See his blubber — at his gills
What a world of drink he swills,
From his trunk as from a spout,
Which next moment he pours out.
    Such his person — next declare,
Muse, who his companions are.
Every fish of generous kind
Scuds aside or slinks behind;
But about his presence keep
All the Monsters of the Deep;

Mermaids, with their tails and singing
His delighted fancy stinging;
Crooked Dolphins, they surround him,
Dog-like Seals, they fawn around him.
Following hard the progress mark,
Of the intolerant salt sea Shark.
For his solace and relief,
Flat-fish are his courtiers chief.
Last and lowest in his train,
Ink fish (libellers of the main)
Their black liquor shed in spite:
(Such on earth *the things that write*).
In his stomach, some do say,
No good thing can ever stay.
Had it been the fortune of it
To have swallowed that old Prophet,
Three days there he'd not have dwelled,
But in one have been expelled.
Hapless mariners are they,
Who beguiled (as seamen say),
Deeming him some rock or island,
Footing sure, safe spot, and dry land,
Anchor in his scaly rind;
Soon the difference they find —
Sudden plumb he sinks beneath them;
Does to ruthless seas bequeathe them.

Name or title, what has he?
Is he Regent of the sea?
From this difficulty free us,
Buffon, Banks or sage Linnæus.
With his wondrous attributes
Say, what appellation suits?
By his bulk, and by his size,
By his oily qualities,
This (or else my eyesight fails),
This should be the PRINCE OF WHALES.

CHARLES LAMB

Death of a Whale

When the mouse died, there was a sort of pity:
the tiny, delicate creature made for grief.
Yesterday, instead, the dead whale on the reef
drew an excited multitude to the jetty.
How must a whale die to wring a tear?
Lugubrious death of a whale: the big
feast for the gulls and sharks; the tug
of the tide simulating life still there,
until the air, polluted, swings this way
like a door ajar from a slaughterhouse.
Pooh! pooh! spare us, give us the death of a mouse
by its tiny hole; not this in our lovely bay.
— Sorry, we are, too, when a child dies;
but at the immolation of a race, who cries?

JOHN BLIGHT

The Maldive Shark

About the Shark, phlegmatical one,
Pale sot of the Maldive sea,
The sleek little pilot-fish, azure and slim,
How alert in attendance be.
From his saw-pit of mouth, from his charnel of maw
They have nothing of harm to dread,
But liquidly glide on his ghastly flank
Or before his Gorgonian head;
Or lurk in the port of serrated teeth
In white triple tiers of glittering gates,
And there find a haven when peril's abroad,
An asylum in jaws of the Fates!

[280]

They are friends; and friendly they guide him to prey
Yet never partake of the treat —
Eyes and brains to the dotard lethargic and dull,
Pale ravener of horrible meat.

HERMAN MELVILLE

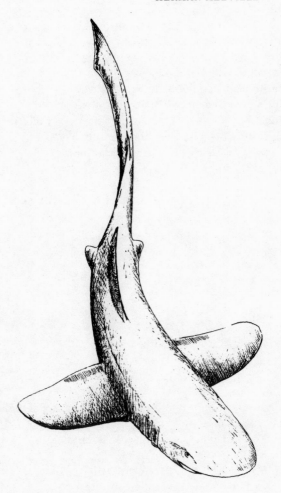

Section 8
MISCELLANEOUS

On a Drop of Dew

See how the orient dew,
Shed from the bosom of the morn
   Into the blowing roses,
Yet careless of its mansion new;
For the clear region where 'twas born
   Round in itself incloses:
   And in its little globe's extent,
Frames as it can its native element.
   How it the purple flower does slight,
     Scarce touching where it lies,
   But gazing back upon the skies,
     Shines with a mournful light;
       Like its own tear,
Because so long divided from the sphere.
   Restless it rolls and unsecure,
     Trembling lest it grow impure:
Till the warm sun pity its pain,
And to the skies exhale it back again.
     So the soul, that drop, that ray
Of the clear fountain of eternal day,
Could it within the human flower be seen,
     Remembering still its former height,
     Shuns the sweet leaves and blossoms green:
     And, recollecting its own light,
Does, in its pure and circling thoughts, express
The greater Heaven in an Heaven less.
    In how coy a figure wound,
    Every way it turns away:
    So the world excluding round,
    Yet receiving in the day.
    Dark beneath, but bright above:
    Here disdaining, there in love.
How loose and easy hence to go:
How girt and ready to ascend.
Moving but on a point below,
It all about does upwards bend.

Such did the manna's sacred dew distil;
White, and entire, though congealed and chill.
   Congealed on earth: but does, dissolving, run
   Into the glories of the Almighty Sun.

ANDREW MARVELL

from

Windsor Forest

When milder autumn summer's heat succeeds,
And in the new-shorn field the partridge feeds,
Before his lord the ready spaniel bounds,
Panting with hope, he tries the furrowed grounds;
But when the tainted gales the game betray,
Couched close he lies, and meditates the prey;
Secure they trust th'unfaithful field beset,
Till hov'ring o'er them sweeps the swelling net.
Thus (if small things we may with great compare)
When Albion sends her eager sons to war,
Some thoughtless town, with ease and plenty blest,
Near, and more near, the closing lines invest;
Sudden they seize th'amazed, defenceless prize,
And high in air Britannia's standard flies.
   See! from the brake the whirring pheasant springs,
And mounts exulting on triumphant wings:
Short is his joy; he feels the fiery wound,
Flutters in blood, and panting beats the ground.
Ah! what avail his glossy, varying dyes,
His purple crest, and scarlet-circled eyes,
The vivid green his shining plumes unfold,
His painted wings, and breast that flames with gold?
   Nor yet, when moist Arcturus clouds the sky,
The woods and fields their pleasing toils deny.
To plains with well-breathed beagles we repair,
And trace the mazes of the circling hare:

[286]

Beasts, urged by us, their fellow-beasts pursue,
And learn of man each other to undo.
With slaught'ring guns th'unwearied fowler roves,
When frosts have whitened all the naked groves;
Where doves in flocks the leafless trees o'ershade,
And lonely woodcocks haunt the wat'ry glade.
He lifts the tube, and levels with his eye;
Straight a short thunder breaks the frozen sky:
Oft, as in airy rings they skim the heath,
The clam'rous lapwings feel the leaden death:
Oft, as the mounting larks their notes prepare,
They fall, and leave their little lives in air.

ALEXANDER POPE

Ode to Evening

If aught of oaten stop, or pastoral song,
May hope, chaste Eve, to soothe thy modest ear,
   Like thy own solemn springs,
   Thy springs and dying gales;

O nymph reserved, while now the bright-hair'd sun
Sits in yon western tent, whose cloudy shirts,
   With brede ethereal wove,
   O'erhang his wavy bed:

Now air is hush'd save where the weak-eyed bat
With a short shrill shriek flits by on leathern wing,
   Or where the beetle winds
   His small but sullen horn,

As oft he rises, midst the twilight path
Against the pilgrim borne in heedless hum:
   Now teach me, maid composed,
   To breath some softened strain,

Whose numbers, stealing through thy dark'ning vale,
May not unseemly with its stillness suit,
 As, musing slow, I hail
 Thy genial loved return!

For when thy folding-star arising shows
His paly circlet, at his warning lamp
 The fragrant hours, and elves
 Who slept in buds the day,

And many a nymph who wreathes her brows with sedge,
And sheds the freshening dew, and, lovelier still,
 The pensive pleasures sweet,
 Prepare thy shadowy car:

Then lead, calm votaress, where some sheety lake
Cheers the lone heath, or some tome-hallow'd pile,
 Or upland fallows grey
 Reflect its last cool gleam.

Or if chill blustering winds, or driving rain,
Prevent my willing feet, be mine the hut
 That from the mountain's side
 Views wilds and swelling floods,

And hamlets brown, and dim-discover'd spires,
And hears their simple bell, and marks o'er all
 Thy dewy fingers draw
 The gradual dusky veil.

While Spring shall pour his show'rs, as oft he wont,
And bathe thy breathing tresses, meekest Eve!
 While Summer loves to sport
 Beneath thy lingering light;

While sallow Autumn fills thy lap with leaves,
Or Winter, yelling through the troublous air,
 Affrights thy shrinking train,
 And rudely rends thy robes:

So long, regardful of thy quiet rule,
Shall Fancy, Friendship, Science, rose-lipp'd Health
  Thy gentlest influence own,
  And hymn thy favourite name!

WILLIAM COLLINS

The Naturalist's
Summer Evening Walk

When day declining sheds a milder gleam,
What time the mayfly haunts the pool or stream;
When the still owl skims round the grassy mead,
What time the timorous hare limps forth to feed;
Then be the time to steal adown the vale,
And listen to the vagrant cuckoo's tale,
To hear the clamorous curlew call his mate:
Or the soft quail his tender pain relate;
To see the swallow sweep the dark'ning plain
Belated, to support her infant train;
To mark the swift in rapid giddy ring
Dash round the steeple, unsubdued of wing:
Amusive birds! — say where your hid retreat
When the frost rages and the tempests beat;
Whence your return, by such nice instinct led,
When spring, soft season, lifts her bloomy head?
Such baffled searches mock men's prying pride,
The God of Nature is your secret guide!
    While deep'ning shades obscure the face of day,
To yonder bench, leaf-sheltered, let us stray,
Till blended objects fail the swimming sight,
And all the fading landscape sinks in night;
To hear the drowsy dor come brushing by
With buzzing wing, or the shrill cricket cry;
To see the feeding bat glance through the wood;
To catch the distant falling of the flood;

While o'er the cliff th'awakened churn owl hung,
Through the still gloom protracts his chattering song;
While high in air, and poised upon his wings,
Unseen, the soft enamoured wood lark sings:
These, Nature's works, the curious mind employ,
Inspire a soothing melancholy joy:
As fancy warms, a pleasing kind of pain
Steals o'er the cheek, and thrills the creeping vein!

Each rural sight, each sound, each smell combine;
The tinkling sheep bell, or the breath of kine;
The new-mown hay that scents the swelling breeze,
Or cottage chimney smoking through the trees.

The chilling night dews fall: away, retire;
For see, the glowworm lights her amorous fire!
Thus, ere night's veil had half obscured the sky,
Th'impatient damsel hung her lamp on high:
True to the signal, by love's meteor led,
Leander hastened to his Hero's bed.

GILBERT WHITE

Progress of Evening

From yonder wood, mark blue-eyed Eve proceed:
First through the deep and warm and secret glens,
Through the pale glimmering privet-scented lane,
And through those alders by the river-side:
Now the soft dust impedes her, which the sheep
Have hollow'd out beneath their hawthorn shade.
But ah! look yonder! see a misty tide
Rise up the hill, lay low the frowning grove,
Enwrap the gay white mansion, sap its sides
Until they sink and melt away like chalk;
Now it comes down against our village-tower,
Covers its base, floats o'er its arches, tears
The clinging ivy from the battlements,
Mingles in broad embrace the obdurate stone,
(All one vast ocean) and goes swelling on
In slow and silent, dim and deepening waves.

WALTER SAVAGE LANDOR

from

The Prelude

It was a summer's night, a close warm night,
Wan, dull and glaring, with a dripping mist
Low-hung and thick that covered all the sky,
Half threatening storm and rain; but on we went
Unchecked, being full of heart and having faith
In our tried pilot. Little could we see
Hemmed round on every side with fog and damp,
And, after ordinary travellers' chat
With our conductor, silently we sank
Each into commerce with his private thoughts:

[291]

Thus did we breast the ascent, and by myself
Was nothing either seen or heard the while
Which took me from my musings, save that once
The shepherd's cur did to his own great joy
Unearth a hedgehog in the mountain crags
Round which he made a barking turbulent.
This small adventure, for even such it seemed
In that wild place and at the dead of night,
Being over and forgotten, on we wound
In silence as before. With forehead bent
Earthward, as if in opposition set
Against an enemy, I panted up
With eager pace, and no less eager thoughts.
Thus might we wear perhaps an hour away,
Ascending at loose distance each from each,
And I, as chanced, the foremost of the band;
When at my feet the ground appeared to brighten,
And with a step or two seemed brighter still;
Nor had I time to ask the cause of this,
For instantly a light upon the turf
Fell like a flash: I looked about, and lo!
The Moon stood naked in the heavens, at height
Immense above my head, and on the shore
I found myself of a huge sea of mist,
Which, meek and silent, rested at my feet.
A hundred hills their dusky backs upheaved
All over this still ocean; and beyond,
Far, far beyond, the vapours shot themselves,
In headlands, tongues, and promontory shapes,
Into the sea, the real sea, that seemed
To dwindle, and give up its majesty,
Usurped upon as far as sight could reach.
Meanwhile, the Moon looked down upon this show
In single glory, and we stood, the mist
Touching our very feet; and from the shore
At distance not the third part of a mile
Was a blue chasm; a fracture in the vapour,
A deep and gloomy breathing-place through which
Mounted the roar of waters, torrents, streams
Innumerable, roaring with one voice!

The universal spectacle throughout
Was shaped for admiration and delight,
Grand in itself alone, but in the breach
Through which the homeless voice of waters rose,
That dark deep thoroughfare, had Nature lodged
The soul, the imagination of the whole.

WILLIAM WORDSWORTH

This Lime-tree Bower my Prison

(Addressed to Charles Lamb,
of the India House, London)

In the June of 1797 some long-expected friends paid a visit to the author's cottage; and on the morning of their arrival, he met with an accident, which disabled him from walking during the whole time of their stay. One evening, when they had left him for a few hours, he composed the following lines in the garden-bower.

Well, they are gone, and here must I remain,
This lime-tree bower my prison! I have lost
Beauties and feelings, such as would have been
Most sweet to my remembrance even when age
Had dimm'd mine eyes to blindness! They, meanwhile,
Friends, whom I never more may meet again,
On springy heath, along the hill-top edge,
Wander in gladness, and wind down, perchance,
To that still roaring dell, of which I told;
The roaring dell, o'erwooded, narrow, deep,
And only speckled by the mid-day sun;
Where its slim trunk the ash from rock to rock
Flings arching like a bridge; — that branchless ash,
Unsunn'd and damp, whose few poor yellow leaves
Ne'er tremble in the gale, yet tremble still,
Fann'd by the water-fall! and there my friends
Behold the dark green file of long lank weeds,
That all at once (a most fantastic sight!)
Still nod and drip beneath the dripping edge
Of the blue clay-stone.

                  Now, my friends emerge
Beneath the wide wide Heaven — and view again
The many-steepled tract magnificent
Of hilly fields and meadows, and the sea,
With some fair bark, perhaps, whose sails light up
The slip of smooth clear blue betwixt two Isles
Of purple shadow! Yes! they wander on

In gladness all; but thou, methinks, most glad,
My gentle-hearted Charles! for thou hast pined
And hunger'd after Nature, many a year,
In the great City pent, winning thy way
With sad yet patient soul, through evil and pain
And strange calamity! Ah! slowly sink
Behind the western ridge, thou glorious Sun!
Shine in the slant beams of the sinking orb,
Ye purple heath-flowers! richlier burn, ye clouds!
Live in the yellow light, ye distant groves!
And kindle, thou blue Ocean! So my friend
Struck with deep joy may stand, as I have stood,
Silent with swimming sense; yea, gazing round
On the wide landscape, gaze till all doth seem
Less gross than bodily; and of such hues
As veil the Almighty Spirit, when yet he makes
Spirits perceive his presence.

               A delight
Comes sudden on my heart, and I am glad
As I myself were there! Nor in this bower,
This little lime-tree bower, have I not mark'd
Much that has sooth'd me. Pale beneath the blaze
Hung the transparent foliage; and I watch'd
Some broad and sunny leaf, and lov'd to see
The shadow of the leaf and stem above
Dappling its sunshine! And that walnut-tree
Was richly ting'd, and a deep radiance lay
Full on the ancient ivy, which usurps
Those fronting elms, and now, with blackest mass
Makes their dark branches gleam a lighter hue
Through the late twilight: and though now the bat
Wheels silent by, and not a swallow twitters,
Yet still the solitary humble-bee
Sings in the bean-flower! Henceforth I shall know
That Nature ne'er deserts the wise and pure;
No plot so narrow, be but Nature there,
No waste so vacant, but may well employ
Each faculty of sense, and keep the heart
Awake to Love and Beauty! and sometimes

'Tis well to be bereft of promis'd good,
That we may lift the soul, and contemplate
With lively joy the joys we cannot share.
My gentle-hearted Charles! when the last rook
Beat its straight path along the dusky air
Homewards, I blest it! deeming its black wing
(Now a dim speck, now vanishing in light)
Had cross'd the mighty Orb's dilated glory,
While thou stood'st gazing; or, when all was still,
Flew creeking o'er thy head, and had a charm
For thee, my gentle-hearted Charles, to whom
No sound is dissonant which tells of Life.

SAMUEL TAYLOR COLERIDGE

from

Childe Harold's Pilgrimage

from Canto III

LXXXVI

It is the hush of night, and all between
Thy margin and the mountains, dusk, yet clear,
Mellow'd and mingling, yet distinctly seen,
Save darken'd Jura, whose capt heights appear
Precipitously steep; and drawing near,
There breathes a living fragrance from the shore,
Of flowers yet fresh with childhood; on the ear
Drops the light drip of the suspended oar,
Or chirps the grasshopper one good-night carol more.

XCVI

Sky, mountains, river, winds, lake, lightnings! ye!
With night, and clouds, and thunder, and a soul
To make these felt and feeling, well may be
Things that have made me watchful; the far roll
Of your departing voices, is the knoll

Of what in me is sleepless, — if I rest.
But where of ye, O tempests! is the goal?
Are ye like those within the human breast?
Or do ye find, at length, like eagles, some high nest?

from Canto IV

XXVII

The moon is up, and yet it is not night;
Sunset divides the sky with her; a sea
Of glory streams along the Alpine height
Of blue Friuli's mountains; Heaven is free
From clouds, but of all colours seems to be, —
Melted to one vast Iris of the West, —
Where the Day joins the past Eternity,
While on the other hand, meek Dian's crest
Floats through the azure air — an island of the blest!

XXVIII

A single star is at her side, and reigns
With her o'er half the lovely heaven; but still
Yon sunny sea heaves brightly, and remains
Roll'd o'er the peak of the far Rhætian hill,
As Day and Night contending were, until
Nature reclaim'd her order: — gently flows
The deep-dyed Brenta, where their hues instil
The odorous purple of a new-born rose,
Which streams upon her stream, and glass'd within it glows,

XXIX

Fill'd with the face of heaven, which, from afar,
Comes down upon the waters; all its hues,
From the rich sunset to the rising star,
Their magical variety diffuse:
And now they change; a paler shadow strews
Its mantle o'er the mountains; parting day
Dies like the dolphin, whom each pang imbues
With a new colour as it gasps away —
The last still loveliest, — till — 'tis gone — and all is gray.

GEORGE GORDON, LORD BYRON

from

The Shepherd's Calendar — January

Blackening through the evening sky,
In clouds the starnels daily fly
To Whittlesea's reed-wooded mere,
And osier holts by rivers near;
Whilst many a mingled swarthy crowd —
Rook, crow, and jackdaw — noising loud,
Fly to and fro to dreary fen,
Dull winter's weary flight again;
They flop on heavy wings away
As soon as morning wakens grey,
And, when the sun sets round and red,
Return to naked woods to bed.
Wood pigeons too in flocks appear,
By hunger tamed from timid fear;
They mid the sheep unstartled steal
And share with them a scanty meal,
Picking the green leaves want bestows
Of turnips sprouting thro' the snows.

JOHN CLARE

[298]

from

Summer Images

I love at early morn, from new-mown swath,
   To see the startled frog his route pursue,
And mark while, leaping o'er the dripping path,
   His bright sides scatter dew;
And early lark that from its bustle flies
   To hail his matin new;
      And watch him to the skies:

And note on hedgerow baulks, in moisture sprent,
   The jetty snail creep from the mossy thorn,
With earnest heed and tremulous intent,
   Frail brother of the morn,
That from the tiny bents and misted leaves
   Withdraws his timid horn,
      And fearful vision weaves:

Or swallow heed on smoke-tanned chimney-top,
   Wont to be first unsealing morning's eye,
Ere yet the bee hath gleaned one wayward drop
   Of honey on his thigh;
To see him seek morn's airy couch to sing,
   Until the golden sky
      Bepaint his russet wing.

JOHN CLARE

from

The Eternity of Nature

All nature's ways are mysteries! Endless youth
Lives in them all, unchangeable as truth.
With the odd number five, her curious laws
Play many freaks, nor once mistake the cause;
For in the cowslip-peeps this very day
Five spots appear, which Time wears not away,
Nor once mistakes in counting — look within
Each peep, and five, nor more nor less, are seen.
So trailing bindweed, with its pinky cup,
Five leaves of paler hue go streaking up;
And many a bird, too, keeps the rule alive,
Laying five eggs, nor more nor less than five.
But flowers, how many own that mystic power,
With five leaves ever making up the flower!
The five-leaved grass, mantling its golden cup
Of flowers — five leaves make all for which I stoop.
The bryony, in the hedge, that now adorns
The tree to which it clings, and now the thorns,
Owns five-starred pointed leaves of dingy white;
Count which I will, all make the number right.
The spreading goose-grass, trailing all abroad
In leaves of silver green about the road —
Five leaves make every blossom all along.
I stoop for many, none are counted wrong.
'Tis Nature's wonder, and her Maker's will,
Who bade earth be, and order owns him still,
As that superior Power, who keeps the key
Of wisdom and of might through all eternity.

JOHN CLARE

Sunrise

The clouds are withdrawn
And their thin-rippled mist,
That stream'd o'er the lawn
To the drowsy-eyed west.
Cold and grey
They slept in the way,
And shrank from the ray
Of the chariot East:
But now they are gone,
And the bounding light
Leaps thro' the bars
Of doubtful dawn;
Blinding the stars,
And blessing the sight;
Shedding delight
On all below;
Glimmering fields,
And wakening wealds,
And rising lark,
And meadows dark,
And idle rills,
And labouring mills,
And far-distant hills
Of the fawn and the doe.
The sun is cheered
And his path is cleared,
As he steps to the air
From his emerald cave,
His heel in the wave,
Most bright and bare;
In the tide of the sky
His radiant hair
From his temples fair
Blown back on high;
As forward he bends,
And upward ascends,

[301]

Timely and true,
To the breast of the blue;
His warm red lips
Kissing the dew,
With sweetened drips
On his flower cupholders;
Every hue
From his gleaming shoulders
Shining anew
With colour sky-born,
As it washes and dips
In the pride of the morn.
Robes of azure,
Fringed with amber,
Fold upon fold
Of purple and gold,
Vine-leaf bloom,
And the grape's ripe gloom,
When season deep
In noontide leisure,
With clustering heap
The tendrils clamber
Full in the face
Of his hot embrace,
Fill'd with the gleams
Of his firmest beams.
Autumn flushes,
Roseate blushes,
Vermeil tinges,
Violet fringes,
Every hue
Of his flower cupholders,
O'er the clear ether
Mingled together,
Shining anew
From his gleaming shoulders!
Circling about
In a coronal rout,
And floating behind,
The way of the wind,

As forward he bends,
And upward ascends,
Timely and true,
To the breast of the blue.
His bright neck curved,
His clear limbs nerved,
Diamond keen
On his front serene,
While each white arm strains
To the racing reins,
As plunging, eyes flashing,
Dripping, and dashing,
His steeds triple grown
Rear up to his throne,
Ruffling the rest
Of the sea's blue breast,
From his flooding, flaming crimson crest

GEORGE MEREDITH

A Sunset

Upon the mountain's edge with light touch resting,
There a brief while the globe of splendour sits
    And seems a creature of the earth; but soon
    More changeful than the Moon,
To wane fantastic his great orb submits,
Or cone or mow of fire: till sinking slowly
Even to a star at length he lessens wholly.

Abrupt, as Spirits vanish, he is sunk!
A soul-like breeze possesses all the wood.
    The boughs, the sprays, have stood
As motionless as stands the ancient trunk!
But every leaf through all the forest flutters,
And deep the cavern of the fountain mutters.

SAMUEL TAYLOR COLERIDGE

[303]

Sunset Wings

To-night this sunset spreads two golden wings
   Cleaving the western sky;
Wing'd too with wind it is, and winnowings
Of birds; as if the day's last hour in rings
   Of strenuous flight must die.

Sun-steepèd in fire, the homeward pinions sway
   Above the dovecote-tops;
And clouds of starlings, ere they rest with day,
Sink, clamorous like mill-waters, at wild play,
   By turns in every copse:

Each tree heart-deep the wrangling rout receives, —
   Save for the whirr within,
You could not tell the starlings from the leaves;
Then one great puff of wings, and the swarm heaves
   Away with all its din.

D. G. ROSSETTI

After Sunset

The vast and solemn company of clouds
Around the Sun's death, lit, incarnadined,
Cool into ashy wan; as Night enshrouds
The level pasture, creeping up behind
Through voiceless vales, o'er lawn and purpled hill
And hazèd mead, her mystery to fulfil.
Cows low from far-off farms; the loitering wind
Sighs in the hedge, you hear it if you will, —
Though all the wood, alive atop with wings
Lifting and sinking through the leafy nooks,
Seethes with the clamour of ten thousand rooks.
Now every sound at length is hush'd away.
These few are sacred moments. One more Day
Drops in the shadowy gulf of bygone things.

WILLIAM ALLINGHAM

The Cloud

I bring fresh showers for the thirsting flowers,
    From the seas and the streams;
I bear light shade for the leaves when laid
    In their noonday dreams.
From my wings are shaken the dews that waken
    The sweet buds every one,
When rocked to rest on their mother's breast,
    As she dances about the sun.
I wield the flail of the lashing hail,
    And whiten the green plains under,
And then again I dissolve it in rain,
    And laugh as I pass in thunder.

I sift the snow on the mountains below,
    And their great pines groan aghast!
And all the night 'tis my pillow white,
    While I sleep in the arms of the blast.
Sublime on the towers of my skiey bowers,
    Lightning my pilot sits;
In a cavern under is fettered the thunder,
    It struggles and howls at fits;
Over earth and ocean, with gentle motion,
    This pilot is guiding me,
Lured by the love of the genii that move
    In the depths of the purple sea;
Over the rills, and the crags, and the hills,
    Over the lakes and the plains,
Wherever he dream, under mountain or stream,
    The Spirit he loves remains;
And I all the while bask in Heaven's blue smile,
    Whilst he is dissolving in rains.

The sanguine Sunrise, with his meteor eyes,
    And his burning plumes outspread,
Leaps on the back of my sailing rack,
    When the morning star shines dead;

As on the jag of a mountain crag,
    Which an earthquake rocks and swings,
An eagle alit one moment may sit
    In the light of its golden wings.
And when Sunset may breathe, from the lit sea beneath,
    Its ardours of rest and of love,
And the crimson pall of eve may fall
    From the depth of Heaven above,
With wings folded I rest, on mine aëry nest,
    As still as a brooding dove.

That orbèd maiden with white fire laden,
    Whom mortals call the Moon,
Glides glimmering o'er my fleece-like floor,
    By the midnight breezes strewn;
And wherever the beat of her unseen feet,
    Which only the angels hear,
May have broken the woof of my tent's thin roof,
    The stars peep behind her and peer;
And I laugh to see them whirl and flee,
    Like a swarm of golden bees,
When I widen the rent in my wind-built tent,
    Till the calm rivers, lakes, and seas,
Like strips of the sky fallen through me on high,
    Are each paved with the moon and these.

I bind the Sun's throne with a burning zone,
    And the Moon's with a girdle of pearl;
The volcanoes are dim, and the stars reel and swim,
    When the whirlwinds my banner unfurl.
From cape to cape, with a bridge-like shape,
    Over a torrent sea,
Sunbeam-proof, I hang like a roof, —
    The mountains its columns be.
The triumphal arch through which I march
    With hurricane, fire, and snow,
When the Powers of the air are chained to my chair,
    Is the million-coloured bow;
The sphere-fire above its soft colours wove,
    While the moist Earth was laughing below.

[306]

I am the daughter of Earth and Water,
    And the nursling of the Sky;
I pass through the pores of the ocean and shores;
    I change, but I cannot die.
For after the rain when with never a stain
    The pavilion of Heaven is bare,
And the winds and sunbeams with their convex gleams
    Build up the blue dome of air,
I silently laugh at my own cenotaph,
    And out of the caverns of rain,
Like a child from the womb, like a ghost from the tomb,
    I arise and unbuild it again.

PERCY BYSSHE SHELLEY

Ode to the West Wind

This poem was conceived and chiefly written in a wood that skirts the Arno, near Florence, and on a day when that tempestuous wind, whose temperature is at once mild and animating, was collecting the vapours which pour down the autumnal rains. They began, as I foresaw, at sunset with a violent tempest of hail and rain, attended by that magnificent thunder and lightning peculiar to the Cisalpine regions.

The phenomenon alluded to at the conclusion of the third stanza is well known to naturalists. The vegetation at the bottom of the sea, of rivers, and of lakes, sympathizes with that of the land in the change of seasons, and is consequently influenced by the winds which announce it. — [SHELLEY'S NOTE.]

I

O wild West Wind, thou breath of Autumn's being,
Thou, from whose unseen presence the leaves dead
Are driven, like ghosts from an enchanter fleeing,

Yellow, and black, and pale, and hectic red,
Pestilence-stricken multitudes: O thou,
Who chariotest to their dark wintry bed

The wingèd seeds, where they lie cold and low,
Each like a corpse within its grave, until
Thine azure sister of the Spring shall blow

Her clarion o'er the dreaming earth, and fill
(Driving sweet buds like flocks to feed in air)
With living hues and odours plain and hill:

Wild Spirit, which art moving everywhere;
Destroyer and preserver; hear, oh, hear!

II

Thou on whose stream, mid the steep sky's commotion,
Loose clouds like earth's decaying leaves are shed,
Shook from the tangled boughs of Heaven and Ocean,

Angels of rain and lightning: there are spread
On the blue surface of thin aëry surge,
Like the bright hair uplifted from the head

Of some fierce Maenad, even from the dim verge
Of the horizon to the zenith's height,
The locks of the approaching storm. Thou dirge

Of the dying year, to which this closing night
Will be the dome of a vast sepulchre,
Vaulted with all thy congregated might

Of vapours, from whose solid atmosphere
Black rain, and fire, and hail will burst: oh, hear!

III

Thou who didst waken from his summer dreams
The blue Mediterranean, where he lay,
Lulled by the coil of his crystàlline streams,

Beside a pumice isle in Baiae's bay,
And saw in sleep old palaces and towers
Quivering within the wave's intenser day,

All overgrown with azure moss and flowers
So sweet, the sense faints picturing them! Thou
For whose path the Atlantic's level powers

Cleave themselves into chasms, while far below
The sea-blooms and the oozy woods which wear
The sapless foliage of the ocean, know

Thy voice, and suddenly grow gray with fear,
And tremble and despoil themselves: oh, hear!

IV

If I were a dead leaf thou mightest bear;
If I were a swift cloud to fly with thee;
A wave to pant beneath thy power, and share

The impulse of thy strength, only less free
Than thou, O uncontrollable! If even
I were as in my boyhood, and could be

The comrade of thy wanderings over Heaven,
As then, when to outstrip thy skiey speed
Scarce seemed a vision; I would ne'er have striven

As thus with thee in prayer in my sore need.
Oh, lift me as a wave, a leaf, a cloud!
I fall upon the thorns of life! I bleed!

A heavy weight of hours has chained and bowed
One too like thee: tameless, and swift, and proud.

V

Make me thy lyre, even as the forest is:
What if my leaves are falling like its own!
The tumult of thy mighty harmonies

Will take from both a deep, autumnal tone,
Sweet though in sadness. Be thou, Spirit fierce,
My spirit! Be thou me, impetuous one!

Drive my dead thoughts over the universe
Like withered leaves to quicken a new birth!
And, by the incantation of this verse,

Scatter, as from an unextinguished hearth
Ashes and sparks, my words among mankind!
Be through my lips to unawakened earth

The trumpet of a prophecy! O, Wind,
If Winter comes, can Spring be far behind?

PERCY BYSSHE SHELLEY

South-west Wind in the Woodland

The silence of preluded song —
Æolian silence charms the woods;
Each tree a harp, whose foliaged strings
Are waiting for the master's touch
To sweep them into storms of joy,
Stands mute and whispers not; the birds
Brood dumb in their foreboding nests,
Save here and there a chirp or tweet,
That utters fear or anxious love,
Or when the ouzel sends a swift
Half warble, shrinking back again
His golden bill, or when aloud

[310]

The storm-cock warns the dusking hills
And villages and valleys round:
For lo, beneath those ragged clouds
That skirt the opening west, a stream
Of yellow light and windy flame
Spreads lengthening southward, and the sky
Begins to gloom, and o'er the ground
A moan of coming blasts creeps low
And rustles in the crisping grass;
Till suddenly with mighty arms
Outspread, that reach the horizon round,
The great South-West drives o'er the earth,
And loosens all his roaring robes
Behind him, over heath and moor.
He comes upon the neck of night,
Like one that leaps a fiery steed
Whose keen black-haunches quivering shine
With eagerness and haste, that needs
No spur to make the dark leagues fly!
Whose eyes are meteors of speed;
Whose mane is as a flashing foam;
Whose hoofs are travelling thunder-shocks; —
He comes, and while his growing gusts,
Wild couriers of his reckless course,
Are whistling from the daggered gorse,
And hurrying over fern and broom,
Midway, far off, he feigns to halt
And gather in his streaming train.

Now, whirring like an eagle's wing
Preparing for a wide blue flight;
Now, flapping like a sail that tacks
And chides the wet bewildered mast;
Now, screaming like an anguish'd thing
Chased close by some down-breathing beak;
Now, wailing like a breaking heart,
That will not wholly break, but hopes
With hope that knows itself in vain;
Now, threatening like a storm-charged cloud
Now, cooing like a woodland dove;

[311]

Now, up again in roar and wrath
High soaring and wide sweeping; now,
With sudden fury dashing down
Full-force on the awaiting woods.

Long waited there, for aspens frail
That twinkle with a silver bell,
To warn the Zephyr of their love,
When danger is at hand, and wake
The neighbouring boughs, surrendering all
Their prophet harmony of leaves,
Had caught his earliest windward thought,
And told it trembling; naked birk
Down showering her dishevelled hair,
And like a beauty yielding up
Her fate to all the elements,
Had swayed in answer; hazels close,
Thick brambles and dark brushwood tufts,
And briared brakes that line the dells
With shaggy beetling brows, had sung
Shrill music, while the tattered flaws
Tore over them, and now the whole
Tumultuous concords, seized at once
With savage inspiration, — pine,
And larch, and beech, and fir, and thorn,
And ash, and oak, and oakling, rave
And shriek, and shout, and whirl, and toss,
And stretch their arms, and split, and crack,
And bend their stems, and bow their heads,
And grind, and groan, and lion-like
Roar to the echo-peopled hills
And ravenous wilds, and crake-like cry
With harsh delight, and cave-like call
With hollow mouth, and harp-like thrill
With mighty melodies, sublime,
From clumps of column'd pines that wave
A lofty anthem to the sky,
Fit music for a prophet's soul —
And like an ocean gathering power,

And murmuring deep, while down below
Reigns calm profound; — not trembling now
The aspens, but like freshening waves
That fall upon a shingly beach; —
And round the oak a solemn roll
Of organ harmony ascends,
And in the upper foliage sounds
A symphony of distant seas.

The voice of nature is abroad
This night; she fills the air with balm;
Her mystery is o'er the land;
And who that hears her now and yields
His being to her yearning tones,
And seats his soul upon her wings,
And broadens o'er the wind-swept world
With her, will gather in the flight
More knowledge of her secret, more
Delight in her beneficence,
Than hours of musing, or the lore
That lives with men could ever give!
Nor will it pass away when morn
Shall look upon the lulling leaves,
And woodland sunshine, Eden-sweet,
Dreams o'er the paths of peaceful shade; —
For every elemental power
Is kindred to our hearts, and once
Acknowledged, wedded, once embraced,
Once taken to the unfettered sense,
Once claspt into the naked life,
The union is eternal.

GEORGE MEREDITH

High Wind

The clouds before him rushed, as they
Were racing home to end the day;
The flying hair of the beeches flew
Out of the East as he went through.

Only the hills unshaken stood.
The lake was tossed into a flood;
She flung her curling wavelets hoar
In wrath on the distracted shore.

Which of the elements hath sinned?
What hath angered thee, O wind?
Thou in all the earth dost see
Nought but it enrageth thee!

MARY COLERIDGE

The Thaw-wind

Thro' the deep drifts the south wind breathed its way
Down to the earth's green face; the air grew warm,
The snow-drops had regain'd their lonely charm,
The world had melted round them in a day:
My full heart long'd for violets — the blue arch
Of heaven — the blackbird's song — but Nature kept
Her stately order — Vegetation slept —
Nor could I force the unborn sweets of March
Upon a winter's thaw. With eyes that brook'd
A narrower prospect than my fancy craved,
Upon the golden aconites I look'd,
And on the leafless willows as they waved —
And on the broad leaved, half-thaw'd ivy-tod,
That glitter'd, dripping down upon the sod.

CHARLES TENNYSON TURNER

[314]

Thaw

Over the land freckled with snow half-thawed
The speculating rooks at their nests cawed
And saw from elm-tops, delicate as flower of grass,
What we below could not see, Winter pass.

EDWARD THOMAS

The Wind's Song

Dull thoughted, walking among the nunneries
Of many a myriad anemones
In the close copses, I grew weary of Spring
Till I emerged and in my wandering
I climbed the down up to a lone pine clump
Of six, the tallest dead, one a mere stump.
On one long stem, branchless and flayed and prone,
I sat in the sun listening to the wind alone,
Thinking there could be no old song so sad
As the wind's song; but later none so glad
Could I remember as that same wind's song
All the time blowing the pine boughs among.
My heart that had been still as the dead tree
Awakened by the West wind was made free.

EDWARD THOMAS

Mist

Low-anchored cloud,
Newfoundland air,
Fountain-head and source of rivers,
Dew-cloth, dream drapery,
And napkin spread by fays;
Drifting meadow of the air,
Where bloom the daisied banks and violets,
And in whose fenny labyrinth
The bittern booms and heron wades;
Spirit of lakes and seas and rivers,
Bear only perfumes and the scent
Of healing herbs to just men's fields!

HENRY DAVID THOREAU

Weathers

I

This is the weather the cuckoo likes,
    And so do I;
When showers betumble the chestnut spikes.
    And nestlings fly:
And the little brown nightingale bills his best,
And they sit outside at 'The Travellers' Rest',
And maids come forth sprig-muslin drest,
And citizens dream of the south and west,
    And so do I.

II

This is the weather the shepherd shuns,
    And so do I:
When beeches drip in browns and duns,
    And thresh, and ply;

[316]

And hill-hid tides throb, throe on throe,
And meadow rivulets overflow.
And drops on gate-bars hang in a row,
And rooks in families homeward go,
     And so do I.

THOMAS HARDY

After Rain

The rain of a night and a day and a night
Stops at the light
Of this pale choked day. The peering sun
Sees what has been done.
The road under the trees has a border new
Of purple hue
Inside the border of bright thin grass:
For all that has
Been left by November of leaves is torn
From hazel and thorn
And the greater trees. Throughout the copse
No dead leaf drops
On grey grass, green moss, burnt-orange fern,
At the wind's return:
The leaflets out of the ash-tree shed
Are thinly spread
In the road, like little black fish, inlaid,
As if they played.
What hangs from the myriad branches down there
So hard and bare
Is twelve yellow apples lovely to see
On one crab-tree.
And on each twig of every tree in the dell
Uncountable
Crystals both dark and bright of the rain
That begins again.

EDWARD THOMAS

A Thunder Shower

And now a cloud, bright, huge and calm,
Rose, doubtful if for bale or balm;
O'ertoppling crags, portentous towers
Appear'd, at beck of viewless powers,
Along a rifted mountain range.
Untraceable and swift in change,
Those glittering peaks, disrupted, spread
To solemn bulks, seen overhead;
The sunshine quench'd, from one dark form
Fumed the appalling light of storm.
Straight to the zenith, black with bale,
The Gipsies' smoke rose deadly pale;
And one wide night of hopeless hue
Hid from the heart the recent blue.
And soon, with thunder crackling loud,
A flash within the formless cloud
Show'd vague recess, projection dim,
Lone sailing rack, and shadowy rim,
Against the whirl of leaves and dust
Kine dropp'd their heads; the tortured gust
Jagg'd and convuls'd the ascending smoke
To mockery of the lightning's stroke.
The blood prick'd, and a blinding flash
And close co-instantaneous crash
Humbled the soul, and the rain all round
Resilient dimm'd the whistling ground,
Nor flagged in force from first to last,
Till, sudden as it came, 'twas past,
Leaving a trouble in the copse
Of brawling birds and tinkling drops.
    Change beyond hope! Far thunder faint
Mutter'd its vast and vain complaint,
And gaps and fractures, fringed with light,
Show'd the sweet skies, with squadrons bright
Of cloudlets, glittering calm and fair
Through gulfs of calm and glittering air.

COVENTRY PATMORE

The Storm is Over

The storm is over, the land hushes to rest:
The tyrannous wind, its strength fordone,
Is fallen back in the west
To couch with the sinking sun.
The last clouds fare
With fainting speed, and their thin streamers fly
In melting drifts of the sky.
Already the birds in the air
Appear again; the rooks return to their haunt,
And one by one,
Proclaiming aloud their care,
Renew their peaceful chant.

Torn and shattered the trees their branches again reset,
They trim afresh the fair
Few green and golden leaves withheld from the storm,
And awhile will be handsome yet.
To-morrow's sun shall caress
Their remnant of loveliness:
In quiet days for a time
Sad Autumn lingering warm
Shall humour their faded prime.

But ah! the leaves of summer that lie on the ground!
What havoc! The laughing timbrels of June,
That curtained the birds' cradles, and screened their song,
That sheltered the cooing doves at noon,
Of airy fans the delicate throng, —
Torn and scattered around:
Far out afield they lie,
In the watery furrows die,
In grassy pools of the flood they sink and drown,
Green-golden, orange, vermilion, golden and brown,
The high year's flaunting crown
Shattered and trampled down.

The day is done: the tired land looks for night:
She prays to the night to keep
In peace her nerves of delight:
While silver mist upstealeth silently,
And the broad cloud-driving moon in the clear sky
Lifts o'er the firs her shining shield,
And in her tranquil light
Sleep falls on forest and field.
See! sleep hath fallen: the trees are asleep:
The night is come. The land is wrapt in sleep.

ROBERT BRIDGES

The Lofty Sky

To-day I want the sky,
The tops of the high hills,
Above the last man's house,
His hedges, and his cows,
Where, if I will, I look
Down even on sheep and rook,
And of all things that move
See buzzards only above: —
Past all trees, past furze
And thorn, where nought deters
The desire of the eye
For sky, nothing but sky.
I sicken of the woods
And all the multitudes
Of hedge-trees. They are no more
Than weeds upon this floor
Of the river of air
Leagues deep, leagues wide, where
I am like a fish that lives
In weeds and mud and gives
What's above him no thought.
I might be a tench for aught

[320]

That I can do to-day
Down on the wealden clay.
Even the tench has days
When he floats up and plays
Among the lily leaves
And sees the sky, or grieves
Not if he nothing sees:
While I, I know that trees
Under the lofty sky
Are weeds, fields mud, and I
Would arise and go far
To where the lilies are.

EDWARD THOMAS

In Harmony with Nature

To a Preacher

"In harmony with Nature?" Restless fool,
Who with such heat dost preach what were to thee,
When true, the last impossibility —
To be like Nature strong, like Nature cool!

Know, man hath all which Nature hath, but more,
And in that *more* lie all his hopes of good.
Nature is cruel, man is sick of blood;
Nature is stubborn, man would fain adore;

Nature is fickle, man hath need of rest;
Nature forgives no debt, and fears no grave;
Man would be mild, and with safe conscience blest

Man must begin, know this, where Nature ends;
Nature and man can never be fast friends.
Fool, if thou canst not pass her, rest her slave!

MATTHEW ARNOLD

Cold-blooded Creatures

Man, the egregious egoist
(In mystery the twig is bent),
Imagines, by some mental twist,
That he alone is sentient

Of the intolerable load
Which on all living creatures lies,
Nor stoops to pity in the toad
The speechless sorrow of its eyes.

He asks no questions of the snake,
Nor plumbs the phosphorescent gloom
Where lidless fishes, broad awake,
Swim staring at a night-mare doom.

ELINOR WYLIE

To Nature

It may indeed be phantasy, when I
    Essay to draw from all created things
    Deep, heartfelt, inward joy that closely clings;
And trace in leaves and flowers that round me lie
Lessons of love and earnest piety.
    So let it be; and if the wide world rings
    In mock of this belief, it brings
Nor fear, nor grief, nor vain perplexity.
So will I build my altar in the fields,
    And the blue sky my fretted dome shall be,
And the sweet fragrance that the wild flower yields
    Shall be the incense I will yield to Thee,
Thee only God! and thou shalt not despise
Even me, the priest of this poor sacrifice.

SAMUEL TAYLOR COLERIDGE

Earth to Earth

Where the region grows without a lord,
   Between the thickets emerald-stoled,
In the woodland bottom the virgin sward,
   The cream of the earth, through depths of mold
   O'erflowing wells from secret cells,
While the moon and the sun keep watch and ward,
   And the ancient world is never old.

Here, alone, by the grass-green hearth
   Tarry a little: the mood will come!
Feel your body a part of earth;
   Rest and quicken your thought at home;
   Take your ease with the brooding trees;
Join in their deep-down silent mirth
   The crumbling rock and the fertile loam.

Listen and watch! The wind will sing;
   And the day go out by the western gate;
The night come up on her darkling wing;
   And the stars with flaming torches wait.
   Listen and see! And love and be
The day and the night and the world-wide thing
   Of strength and hope you contemplate.

No lofty Patron of Nature! No;
   Nor a callous devotee of Art!
But the friend and the mate of the high and the low,
   And the pal to take the vermin's part,
   Your inmost thought divinely wrought,
In the grey earth of your brain aglow
   With the red earth burning in your heart.

JOHN DAVIDSON

Dun-colour

Subtle almost beyond thought are these dim colours,
The mixed, the all-including, the pervasive,
Earth's own delightful livery, banqueting
The eye with dimness that includes all brightness;
Complexity which the mind sorts out, as the sunlight
Resolves into many purities the mingled
Dun fleeces of the moorland; the quartz sparkles,
The rosy heath glows, the mineral-like mosses
And the heathbells and the myriad lichens
Start each into the eye a separate splendour:
So in the mind's sun bloom the dim dun-colours.

The dry vermilion glow of familiar redbreast
Is not his real glory: that is the greenish,
Light-toned, light-dissembling, eye-deceiving
Dun of his smooth-sloped back, and on his belly
The whitish dun is laid to deceive the shadow:
In the dear linnet the olive-dun is lovely,
And the primrose-duns in the yellowhammer: but
    most beguiling,
Perhaps because of the perfect shape, is the ash-dun,
That quietest, most urbane, unprofaneable colour
Reserved as her livery of beauty to the hedge-sparrow.
There is a royal azure in her blood,
As her eggs prove, and in her nature gold,
For her children's throats are kingcups; but she veils them,
Mingled and blended, in her rare dun-colour.

For the rose-duns, and the blue-duns, look to the finches:
For the clear clear brown-duns, to the fallow deer
(How the sudden tear smarts in the eye wearied of cities)
And for all these and more to the many toadstools,
Which alone have the violet-dun, livid yet lovely:
But the most delicate duns are seen in the gentle
Monkeys from the great forests, the silvan spirits:
Wonderful! that these, almost our brothers,
Should be dressed so rarely, in sulphurous-dun and greenish:
O that a man had grassy hair like these dryads!
O that I too were attired in such dun-colours!

RUTH PITTER

[324]

Song

Swamps of wild rush-beds, and sloughs' squashy traces,
   Grounds of rough fallows with thistle and weed,
Flats and low valleys of kingcups and daisies,
   Sweetest of subjects are ye for my reed:
Ye commons left free in the rude rags of nature,
   Ye brown heaths beclothed in furze as ye be,
My wild eye in rapture adores every feature,
   Ye are dear as this heart in my bosom to me.

O native endearments! I would not forsake ye,
   I would not forsake ye for sweetest of scenes;
For sweetest of gardens that nature could make me,
   I would not forsake ye, dear valleys and greens:
Tho' nature ne'er dropt ye a cloud-resting mountain,
   Nor waterfalls tumble their music so free;
Had nature denied ye a bush, tree, or fountain,
   Ye still had been lov'd as an Eden by me.

And long, my dear valleys, long, long may ye flourish,
  Though rush-beds and thistles make most of your pride;
May showers never fail the green's daisies to nourish,
  Nor suns dry the fountain that rills by its side.
Your skies may be gloomy, and misty your mornings,
  Your flat swampy valleys unwholesome may be;
Still, refuse of nature, without her adornings
  Ye are dear as this heart in my bosom to me.

JOHN CLARE

Where the Lilies used to Spring

When the place was green with the shaky grass,
  And the windy trees were high;
When the leaflets told each other tales,
  And stars were in the sky;
When the silent crows hid their ebon beaks
  Beneath their ruffled wing —
Then the fairies watered the glancing spot
  Where the lilies used to spring!

When the sun is high in the summer sky,
  And the lake is deep with clouds;
When gadflies bite the prancing kine,
  And light the lark enshrouds —
Then the butterfly, like a feather dropped
  From the tip of an angel's wing,
Floats wavering on to the glancing spot
  Where the lilies used to spring!

When the wheat is shorn and the burns run brown,
  And the moon shines clear at night;
When wains are heaped with rustling corn,
  And the swallows take their flight;

When the trees begin to cast their leaves,
   And the birds, new-feathered, sing —
Then comes the bee to the glancing spot
   Where the lilies used to spring!

When the sky is grey and the trees are bare,
   And the grass is long and brown,
And black moss clothes the soft damp thatch,
   And the rain comes weary down,
And countless droplets on the pond
   Their widening orbits ring —
Then bleak and cold is the silent spot
   Where the lilies used to spring!

DAVID GRAY

The Call of the Wild

Have you gazed on naked grandeur where there's nothing else to
   gaze on,
   Set pieces and drop-curtain scenes galore,
Big mountains heaved to heaven, which the blinding sunsets
   blazon,
   Black canyons where the rapids rip and roar?
Have you swept the visioned valley with the green stream streaking
   through it,
   Searched the Vastness for a something you have lost?
Have you strung your soul to silence? Then for God's sake go and
   do it;
   Hear the challenge, learn the lesson, pay the cost.

Have you wandered in the wilderness, the sagebrush desolation,
   The bunch-grass levels where the cattle graze?
Have you whistled bits of rag-time at the end of all creation,
   And learned to know the desert's little ways?

Have you camped upon the foothills, have you galloped o'er the
ranges,
Have you roamed the arid sun-lands through and through?
Have you chummed up with the mesa? Do you know its moods and
changes?
Then listen to the wild — it's calling you.

Have you known the Great White Silence, not a snow-gemmed
twig aquiver?
(Eternal truths that shame our soothing lies.)
Have you broken trail on snowshoes? mushed your huskies up the
river,
Dared the unknown, led the way, and clutched the prize?
Have you marked the map's void spaces, mingled with the mongrel
races,
Felt the savage strength of brute in every thew?
And though grim as hell the worst is, can you round it off with
curses?
Then hearken to the Wild — it's wanting you.

Have you suffered, starved and triumphed, groveled down, yet
grasped at glory,
Grown bigger in the bigness of the whole?
"Done things" just for the doing, letting babblers tell the story,
Seeing through the nice veneer the naked soul?
Have you seen God in His splendors, heard the text that nature
renders?
(You'll never hear it in the family pew.)
The simple things, the true things, the silent men who do
things —
Then listen to the Wild — it's calling you.

They have cradled you in custom, they have primed you with
their preaching,
They have soaked you in convention through and through;
They have put you in a showcase; you're a credit to their
teaching —
But can't you hear the Wild? — it's calling you.

Let us probe the silent places, let us seek what luck betide us;
    Let us journey to a lonely land I know.
There's a whisper on the night-wind, there's a star agleam to
    guide us,
    And the Wild is calling, calling . . . let us go.

ROBERT SERVICE

The Voice of Nature

There is a language wrote on earth and sky
By God's own pen in silent majesty;
There is a voice that's heard and felt and seen
In spring's young shades and summer's endless green;
There is a book of poesy and spells
In which that voice in sunny splendour dwells;
There is a page in which that voice aloud
Speaks music to the few and not the crowd;
Though no romantic scenes my feet have trod,
The voice of nature as the voice of God
Appeals to me in every tree and flower,
Breathing his glory, magnitude and power.
In nature's open book I read, and see
Beauty's rich lesson in this seeming-pea;
Crowds see no magic in the trifling thing;
Pshaw! 'tis a weed, and millions came with spring.
I hear rich music wheresoe'er I look,
But heedless worldlings chide the brawling brook;
And that small lark between me and the sky
Breathes sweetest strains of morning's melody;
Yet by the heedless crowd 'tis only heard
As the small warbling of a common bird
That o'er the plough teams hails the morning sun;
They see no music from such magic won.
Yet I see melody in nature's laws,
Or do I dream? — still wonder bids me pause:

[329]

I pause, and hear a voice that speaks aloud:
'Tis not on earth nor in the thundercloud;
The many look for sound — 'tis silence speaks,
And song like sunshine from her rapture breaks.
I hear it in my bosom ever near;
'Tis in these winds, and they are everywhere.
It casts around my vision magic spells
And makes earth heaven where poor fancy dwells.
I read its language, and its speech is joy;
So, without teaching when a lonely boy,
Each weed to me did happy tidings bring,
And laughing daisies wrote the name of spring,
And God's own language unto nature given
Seemed universal as the light of heaven
And common as the grass upon the plain,
That all may read and meet with joy again,
Save the unheeding heart that, like the tomb,
Shuts joy in darkness and forbids its bloom.

JOHN CLARE

The Voice of Nature

I stand on the cliff and watch the veiled sun paling
  A silver field afar in the mournful sea,
The scourge of the surf, and plaintive gulls sailing
  At ease on the gale that smites the shuddering lea:
    Whose smile severe and chaste
  June never hath stirred to vanity, nor age defaced.
In lofty thought strive, O spirit, for ever:
In courage and strength pursue thine own endeavour.

Ah! if it were only for thee, thou restless ocean
  Of waves that follow and roar, the sweep of the tides;
Wer't only for thee, impetuous wind, whose motion
  Precipitate all o'errides, and turns, nor abides:
    For you sad birds and fair,
  Or only for thee, bleak cliff, erect in the air;

[330]

Then well could I read wisdom in every feature,
O well should I understand the voice of Nature.

But far away, I think, in the Thames valley,
    The silent river glides by flowery banks:
And birds sing sweetly in branches that arch an alley
    Of cloistered trees, moss-grown in their ancient ranks:
        Where if a light air stray,
        'Tis laden with hum of bees and scent of may.
Love and peace be thine, O spirit, for ever:
Serve thy sweet desire: despise endeavour.

And if it were only for thee, entranced river,
    That scarce dost rock the lily on her airy stem,
Or stir a wave to murmur, or a rush to quiver;
    Wer't but for the woods, and summer asleep in them:
        For you my bowers green,
        My hedges of rose and woodbine, with walks between,
Then well could I read wisdom in every feature,
O well should I understand the voice of Nature.

ROBERT BRIDGES

Reason for not writing
Orthodox Nature Poetry

The January sky is deep and calm.
The mountain sprawls in comfort, and the sea
Sleeps in the crook of that enormous arm.

And Nature from a simple recipe —
Rocks, water, mist, a sunlit winter's day —
Has brewed a cup whose strength has dizzied me.

So little beauty is enough to pay;
The heart so soon yields up its store of love,
And where you love you cannot break away.

[331]

So sages never found it hard to prove
Nor prophets to declare in metaphor
That God and Nature must be hand in glove.

And this became the basis of their lore.
Then later poets found it easy going
To give the public what they bargained for,

And like a spectacled curator showing
The wares of his museum to the crowd,
They yearly waxed more eloquent and knowing

More slick, more photographic, and more proud:
From Tennyson with notebook in his hand
(His truth to Nature fits him like a shroud)

To moderns who devoutly hymn the land.
So be it: each is welcome to his voice;
They are a gentle, if a useless, band.

But leave me free to make a sterner choice;
Content, without embellishment, to note
How little beauty bids the heart rejoice,

How little beauty catches at the throat,
Simply, I love this mountain and this bay
With love that I can never speak by rote,

And where you love you cannot break away.

JOHN WAIN

LIST OF AUTHORS

Allingham, William (1824–89)
Amabile, George (b. 1936)
Anne, Countess of Winchilsea (1661–1720)
Anonymous
Arnold, Matthew (1822–88)

Barnes, William (1801–86)
Barnfield, Richard (1574–1627)
Beddoes, Thomas Lovell (1803–49)
Benson, A. C. (1862–1925)
Birney, Earle (b. 1904)
Blake, William (1757–1827)
Blight, John (b. 1913)
Blunden, Edmund (1896–1974)
Bridges, Robert (1844–1930)
Brontë, Charlotte (1816–55)
Brooke, Rupert (1887–1915)
Bryant, William Cullen (1794–1878)
Bunyan, John (1628–88)
Burns, Robert (1759–96)
Byron, Lord (1788–1824)

Campbell, Thomas (1777–1844)
Campbell, Wilfred (1861–1918)
Clare, John (1793–1864)
Clough, A. H. (1819–61)
Coleridge, Hartley (1796–1849)
Coleridge, Mary (1861–1907)
Coleridge, Samuel Taylor (1772–1834)
Collins, William (1721–59)
Cotton, Charles (1630–87)
Cowley, Abraham (1618–67)
Cowper, William (1731–1800)
Crane, Hart (1899–1932)

Davidson, John (1837–1909)
De la Mare, Walter (1871–1956)
Dickens, Charles (1812–70)

[333]

Dickinson, Emily (1830–86)
Dickinson, Patric (b. 1914)
Dixon, Richard Watson (1833–1900)
Drummond, William (1585–1649)

Emerson, Ralph Waldo (1803–82)

Freneau, Philip (1752–1832)
Frost, Robert (1874–1963)

Gay, John (1685–1732)
Gibbons, Orlando (1583–1625)
Gray, David (1838–61)

Hardy, Owen (b. 1946)
Hardy, Thomas (1840–1928)
Harpur, Charles (1813–68)
Hayne, Paul Hamilton (1830–86)
Herrick, Robert (1591–1674)
Heyrick, Thomas (1649–94)
Hogg, James (1770–1835)
Hood, Thomas (1799–1845)
Hopkins, Gerard Manley (1844–89)
Housman, A. E. (1859–1936)
Hughes, Ted (b. 1930)
Hulme, T. E. (1883–1917)
Hunt, Leigh (1784–1859)

Jeffers, Robinson (1887–1962)

Keats, John (1795–1821)
Kendall, Henry (1841–82)
King, Henry (1592–1669)

Lamb, Charles (1775–1834)
Lampman, Archibald (1861–99)
Landor, Walter Savage (1775–1864)
Lanier, Sidney (1842–81)
Lawrence, D. H. (1885–1930)
Longfellow, H. W. (1817–82)
Lovelace, Richard (1618–58)
Lowell, James Russell (1819–91)
Lyte, Henry Francis (1793–1847)

Marvell, Andrew (1621–78)
Melville, Herman (1819–91)
Meredith, George (1828–1909)
Meynell, Alice (1847–1922)
Monro, Harold (1879–1932)
Moore, Marianne (1887–1972)

Newbolt, Sir Henry (1862–1938)
North, Christopher (1785–1854)

Palgrave, F. T. (1824–97)
Patmore, Coventry (1823–96)
Pitter, Ruth (b. 1897)
Pope, Alexander (1688–1744)

Rogers, Samuel (1763–1855)
Rossetti, Christina (1830–94)
Rossetti, D. G. (1828–82)

Service, Robert (1874–1958)
Shelley, Percy Bysshe (1792–1822)
Sidney, Sir Philip (1554–86)
Silkin, Jon (b. 1930)
Southey, Robert (1774–1843)
Sterling, George (1869–1926)

Tennyson, Lord Alfred (1809–92)
Thomas, Edward (1878–1917)
Thompson, Francis (1859–1907)
Thomson, James (1700–48)
Thoreau, Henry David (1817–62)
Thwaite, Anthony (b. 1930)
Turner, Charles Tennyson (1808–79)
Turpin, Bob (b. 1943)

Vaughan, Henry (1622–95)

Wade, Thomas (1805–75)
Wain, John (b.1925)
Warren, John Leicester, Lord de Tabley (1835–95)
Warton, Joseph (1722–1800)
Watkins, Vernon (1906–67)
White, Gilbert (1720–93)

LIST OF AUTHORS

Whitman, Walt (1819–92)
Wolcot, John (1738–1819)
Wordsworth, William (1770–1850)
Wylie, Elinor (1885–1928)

Zaturenska, Marya (b. 1902)

ACKNOWLEDGEMENTS

For permission to reproduce copyright material I am indebted to the following:

For *Prairie* by George Amabile from *The Presence of Fire* — used by permission of the Canadian publishers, McClelland & Stewart, Toronto.

For *Slug in Woods* by Earle Birney from *The Collected Poems of Earle Birney*, McClelland & Stewart, Toronto — the author.

For *Death of a Whale* by John Blight from *A Beachcomber's Diary*, Angus & Robertson Publishers — the publishers.

For *The Pike* by Edmund Blunden from *The Waggoner and Other Poems*, Sidgwick & Jackson Ltd — the publishers.

For *The Snail* and *Quack* by Walter de la Mare from *Complete Poems of Walter de la Mare* — the Literary Trustees of Walter de la Mare and the Society of Authors as their representative.

For *There's a certain slant of light, Bee! I'm expecting you!* and *The Bee* by Emily Dickinson from *The Poems of Emily Dickinson*, Harvard University Press — reprinted by permission of the publishers and the Trustees of Amherst College from *The Poems of Emily Dickinson*, edited by Thomas H. Johnson, Cambridge, Mass.: The Belknap Press of Harvard University Press, copyright 1951, © 1955, 1979, 1983 by the President and Fellows of Harvard College.

For *Common Terns* from *The Sailing Race* and *The Redwing* from *The World I See* by Patric Dickinson, both published by Chatto & Windus — the author.

For *Hyla Brook* by Robert Frost from *The Poetry of Robert Frost*, Henry Holt & Company, Inc — copyright 1916, © 1969 by Holt, Rinehart & Winston. Copyright 1944 by Robert Frost. Reprinted from *The Poetry of Robert Frost*, edited by Edward Connery Lathem, by permission of Henry Holt & Company, Inc, Jonathan Cape Ltd and the Estate of Robert Frost.

For *Bittern* and *A Walk on the Machair of North Uist* by Owen Hardy — *Curlew* magazine and the author.

For *A Swallow* by Ted Hughes from *Season Songs*, Faber & Faber Ltd — the publishers and Viking Penguin Inc.

For *Hurt Hawks* by Robinson Jeffers from *The Selected Poetry of Robinson Jeffers*, Random House, Inc — the publishers.

[337]

ACKNOWLEDGEMENTS

For *A Jellyfish* by Marianne Moore from *The Complete Poems of Marianne Moore*, © 1966 by Marianne Moore. All rights reserved. Reprinted by permission of Viking Penguin Inc.

For *Dun-colour* by Ruth Pitter from *Collected Poems*, Cresset Press — Century Hutchinson Publishing Group Ltd.

For *The Pines* and *The Call of the Wild* by Robert Service from *Collected Poems*, Ernest Benn Ltd — © Dodd Mead & Co. Used by permission of the Estate of Robert Service.

For *Moss* by Jon Silkin from *Nature with Man*, Chatto and Windus — the author and Routledge & Kegan Paul plc.

For *Hedgehog* by Anthony Thwaite from *Poems 1953–1983*, Secker & Warburg Ltd — the author.

For *Heron* by Bob Turpin — *Curlew* magazine and the author.

For *Reason for not writing Orthodox Nature Poetry* by John Wain from *A Word Carved on a Sill*, Routledge & Kegan Paul, plc — the author and the publishers.

For *The Curlew* from *Cypress and Acacia* and *The Feather* from *The Lady with the Unicorn* by Vernon Watkins, both published by Faber & Faber Ltd — Mrs Gwen Watkins.

For *The Daisy* by Marya Zaturenska from *The Listening Landscape*, Macmillan Publishing Company — Patrick B. Gregory.

[338]

INDEX OF FIRST LINES